Beat the Clock Cooking

"Take the easy way out of the kitchen!"

By Terrie Macfarlane &
Lisa Rubino

Illustrated by
Brad Blevins

Address all inquiries to:
TeriLee Productions, Inc.
785 Oak Grove Road #E-2
Concord, CA 94518

International Standard Book #0-9654204-7-7
Library of Congress Catalogue Card #96-090562

Printed in the United States of America

Table of Contents

Fasta' Pasta: May . . . Show 4

Quick recipes for the pasta lover who wants a good dish of pasta — and wants it NOW!

No-Host Party: June . . . Show 5

Celebrate in style and cook with ease as these make-ahead, finger snaps are just a pantry away. It's your party — BE there.

Low-Fat Snack Attack: June ... Show 6   45

Got the munchies? You'll delight in every bite of this quick dip and dishes that gratify.

Frozen Assets: August ... Show 9   63

*This cold storage bin is one of your best kitchen helpers. Find new ways
to make these icy packages hot and delicious.*

See Jane Run — the Microwave!

Table of Contents

Acknowledgments

We'd Like to Take This Opportunity to Thank . . .

The two of us agree, it **is** whom — not what — you know that counts. Judging by our long list of thank yous, there have been quite a few we've been able to count on. Starting with the top — God. It's important to us that we express our thanks for grace and mercy. (And the sheer fact that we didn't keel over before this book went to print.) Also for giving us super friends and family.

You may have heard the song, "Stand By Your Man." Well, our men have had to stand by their women, as we shaped and baked our way to the top (of the **stairs** — on production day). They'd set-up, tear down, work on camera or microphone, and bravely taste-test our food experiments. It's "aprons off" to our two special guys, Rich and Scott.

*Speaking of exceptional people — we can't say enough about our two talented associate producers who also stood by us **every** step of the way (literally)*: Brad Blevins and Kathleen Stevens. They are our multi-functioning, dynamic duo. Their professional and creative touch is evident on every page of our book and newsletter, as well as each televised production. Brad's artistic flare and Kathleen's verbal finesse are paired with their kind and gentle hearts. Together they have struggled to unravel, compile and format a year's worth of production notes, interviews and recipes for this book.

They also became adept as "Monday night mediators" for our weekly cookbook meetings. They found patience when we "lost it" and gave us strength when we had no more. They made us laugh at mistakes, push harder, reach higher, give in and forgive.

We are sincerely grateful to: Dan Rubino, John Murray, Michael Tostado, Kathryn Simms, Michael Dillon, Lili Rollins, Robyn Olson, Gina Assoni, Kirstie Macfarlane, Lloy Blevins and our lovable young mascot, Kendra Wilson, for volunteering their time and energy to "The ShortCut Cook."

Our indebtedness is acknowledged to Lyles and Geraldine Pember for their love and support and for **truly believing** in us.

Heartfelt thanks goes to Ed Stokes from Diablo Foods and Steve Rossi of El Monte Cabinets for their generous contributions of supplies and set, respectively.

Recognition is due to our very talented composer, Simon Russell, of Peace Child Productions. He brought our show alive with his snappy, happy theme tunes.

Appreciation goes to Christine Ritter who contributed her artwork during our first year.

We tender thanks to all our guest professionals for their willingness to share their time and expertise with us and our viewers on "The ShortCut Cook" television program.

Grateful mention must be made to Barbara Oleksiw of Oleksiw Creative for her editorial services and her professional suggestions extended in friendship to a couple of novice authors.

Praise goes to the original resident sponsors who helped us bring "The ShortCut Cook" television show to their communities: Pat Cortese, Stan Duford, Rusty and Kaye Assoni and Lee Harcourt.

Our hats are off to all the station and cable system program directors and coordinators who faithfully air our episodes and always have encouraging words.

We'd like to especially thank TCI, Walnut Creek, California, whose elite team of Rob Barry, J. Scott Hayden, James Eldredge and Matt Bolender graciously shot our **first** demo tape (before we even **had** a show!).

In particular, we are grateful to Charly Shepler. Thank you for making "The ShortCut Cook" show possible by opening up the Martinez, California, studio doors and allowing us to "scheme a dream."

A Note to You

We are two hard working women — with too little time to cook. There wasn't a television cooking show that met our everyday needs. So, in 1994 we decided to address this issue and planned a counterattack on the Food Front — over the airwaves!

Come along with us as we share our practical recipes, helpful tips and personal thoughts harvested from our first year of taping "The ShortCut Cook."

A gourmet cookbook this **isn't**. All our recipes were developed from a firsthand, overworked cook's perspective to make the **most** of what you **have** on hand.

"Cookin' Cupboards," found in the appendix, is a review of the time-saving ingredients we use to make all the recipes in this book. We encourage "staple stocking" your pantry to guarantee **no overtime** in the kitchen. This simple step takes the guesswork out of mealtime madness.

Throughout the chapters, you'll find useful and interesting tips gathered from our research, to create those shows, as well as from the guests we featured in each program. (We soon began referring to their spots as "getting professional help.") From chefs and fitness experts to chemists and dietitians, you'll learn the **real scoop**.

A behind-the-scenes tour also awaits you in the Sidelines section of each chapter. Here's where we narrate the frantic fun and flurry of each production day. You'll get an inside look at the upside-down, inside-out world of an unconventional (to say the least) cooking show.

Yours in ShortCuts,

Terrie and *Lisa*

Setting the Stage

It had been about five years since we had taped our last television production (a fitness show). We were now about to "trade in" our sneakers for a miniprocessor and nonstick skillet. From burning up calories to cookin' 'em up! There was just one, minor problem. We didn't have a kitchen set.

*Living up to our reputation as the "Terrible Twos" — the mere lack of scenery couldn't discourage us. We were at it again; dreaming and scheming and **hoping** to beat the odds.*

It didn't matter that we didn't have a stove, running water or even a microwave! We had everything we needed to get started: a great crew, some delicious recipes, an eager host and an impossible dream. We were determined to begin our "do as I say, not as I do" cooking show, by the seat of our pants and the magic of television! So, we gathered up an old plywood stereo console and decorated it with — kitchen stuff: teacups, plates, utensils and plants. The rest was imagination. Kind of like playing house!

We can't wait to share with you the valuable lessons we learned in creating and producing our makin'-due-with-what-ya'-got show. The experience made us a couple of brazen (and braising) broads who can cook anything, anywhere, anytime for anybody. These recipes will show you how. They were created to serve two to four persons, and are formulated to be made and ready to serve in under twenty minutes!

*Right now, WE'RE COOKIN' FOR **YOU**!*

CHICKEN ON THE RUN

Like most everyone these days, you're in a rush and don't have time to whip up fancy dishes. "Get it on the plate and serve it fast," reflects the **real** *world of preparing meals.*

Knowing that people need more time for themselves and want relief from the cooking drudges, we emphasize fresh, canned and convenience foods to help. Our pantry-ready cooking style utilizes your food storage system: refrigerator, freezer and cupboards.

One convenience food, in your supermarket's deli, is a real meal-starter. Buy a roasted chicken. It's already cooked, already seasoned and a great pick up for after work.

Serve it hot from the deli, or add to salads, soups or sandwiches. This time-saving fowl play is fair game for any busy cook.

The hardest part in buying these fellows, is getting them home in one piece. They are that good! Most recipes in this chapter use this ever-ready, deli-prepared chicken.

Here's the skinny: It **costs** *more but* **saves** *time.*

KITCHEN CACCIATORE

"Kitchen Cacciatore" is our signature recipe. This Italian dish, modeled after Chicken Cacciatore, usually takes hours to prepare. Lisa's hurry-up version takes little time to turn out big taste.

1	whole already cooked deli chicken (remove skin, separate into pieces)
15 oz.	can stewed tomatoes, cut up in can
15 oz.	can whole ripe olives, drained
4 $^1/_2$ oz.	can mushrooms, drained (or 8 oz. fresh, see next page)
6 $^1/_2$ oz.	jar marinated artichoke hearts, drained and rinsed (see next page)
$^1/_4$ cup	sherry
2 Tbs.	garlic powder
1 Tbs.	Italian seasonings

In medium to large microwaveable bowl or casserole dish, add all the above ingredients. Microwave 5 minutes on high or until hot.

For a thicker sauce, drain liquid from bowl into a sauce pan. In a separate small bowl, add two ounces cold water and one teaspoon corn starch. Mix well. Add to sauce pan. Stir over medium heat until thickened.

Step Aside

Up and down we go. Who would have thought the road to success would be mostly up hill? Just getting ready for our first in-studio show (and hence ever after) had us exhausted even before the "Lights, Camera, Action" call. We had to unload two cars, a van, a truck then haul equipment and ingredients up two flights of switch-back stairs;

It may be tiny, cramped, dark and claustrophobic, but it's home!

fifteen trips upstairs, fifteen trips down. The sixteenth and last climb had us thanking the Stairmaster, but questioning our sanity.

Our 10' x 16' studio looked like a teenager's bedroom, with floor space reserved for an acrobat. We were stepping over boxes and hunting through grocery bags like scavengers.

The only thing that was clear and obvious was that we needed more time — and there wasn't any. We were still foraging for last-minute ingredients when the director ordered, "Action!" and began the countdown. Lisa is cued to camera one for the start of live-action taping.

Watch and stir — about 2 minutes (if sauce doesn't thicken, add one more teaspoon of corn starch mixed with a little water).

Serve "Kitchen Cacciatore" over polenta (fast cooking — 5 minutes)! Place one slice of Monterey Jack cheese on plate. Place hot polenta on top of cheese. Top with "Cacciatore." Mmm, good!

SHORTCUTS

- *Mix, cook and serve in same microwaveable bowl — for less cleanup.*
- *Use an empty can to "measure" ingredients.*
- *Use a dull table knife to cut up ingredients right in their can when recipes call for anything chopped.*
- *If you prefer using fresh mushrooms, buy them precleaned (and even sliced) from the produce or salad bar section of your supermarket.*
- *By rinsing marinated artichokes before using, you'll consume fewer oil (fat) calories.*

MAMA MIA'S QUICK CHICK

6	skinless, boneless chicken breasts
11 $^1/_8$ oz.	Italian tomato soup
8 oz.	fresh mushrooms, sliced (or 4 oz. can, drained)
1 cup	Monterey Jack or mozzarella cheese
2 Tbs.	garlic powder
1 tsp.	salt (optional)

Preheat oven to 450°. In an 8" x 11" casserole, arrange chicken breasts. Cover with two tablespoons of soup on each piece. Season with garlic and salt. Sprinkle with mushrooms. Bake uncovered at 450° for 15 minutes. Add enough cheese to cover each chicken breast and bake another 3 to 5 minutes. Serve with favorite pasta.

SHORTCUT
* To use up the rest of the soup, add it to your **next** pasta sauce.

Blast-off is seconds away.

"In 5 . . ."

Suddenly Lisa waves to Terrie. She's franticly looking for her main recipe ingredient — the missing chicken — as the floor director continues his countdown.

" . . . 4 . . . 3 . . . 2 . . ."

"Where's the CHICKEN?"

" . . . 1!"

*Lisa's **on air** but the chicken is **NOT**!*

So begins our adventure, in this hide 'n' seek, up-a-creek cooking show.

4

DELI-COOKED CHICKEN

- *Save 1¹/₂ hours of kitchen time by letting someone else do the cooking. The deli-cooked chicken will keep in your fridge for 3 to 5 days.*
- *Removing skin will reduce the fat calories. Chickens in the deli are HOT, so let them cool before you remove the skin.*

SHORTCUTS

- *Hold chicken part in one hand and use a paper towel (in the other hand) to grip and pull off the skin. (Remember to discard bones safely away from pets.) The paper gives extra traction and keeps the skin from slipping.*
- *Now that the skin is removed, just break the chicken apart. No need to dirty a knife.*

ROASTING TIPS

The deli-cooked chicken can be 3¹/₂ times the cost of a raw chicken. So if you would prefer to roast your own chicken:

- Buy **two** 2 to 3 pound roaster chickens. Cooking more than one enables you to have pantry-ready poultry, at your fingertips, for a quick chicken dinner, salad or sandwich.
- Preheat oven to 500°. Rinse chicken in cold water. Drain and pat dry. Place in a shallow roasting pan, breast side down.
- For easy cleanup, line the roasting pan with foil or spray it with nonstick cooking spray.
- Bake at 500° for 30 minutes, uncovered. Reduce heat to 450° and cook another 45 minutes. Pierce breast with fork and make sure juice is clear. Cool and remove skin. Salt and cover with your favorite barbecue sauce. Or, season with garlic powder and dried Italian herbs.

SWIFT LUNCHEON SALADS

Pick a cuisine. Open your cupboard doors and add desired ingredients to leftover, diced chicken and bagged lettuce.

Oriental — Chow mein noodles, sesame seeds and "Oriental Dressing."

Mexican — Tortilla chips, tomatoes, black beans, shredded Cheddar cheese with "2001 Island Dressing."

Californian — Avocado, tomatoes, sprouts, "Sweet Hot Mustard Dressing."

Mediterranean — Feta cheese, Greek olives, tomatoes, garbanzo beans, fresh red onion slices under "Lisa's Italian Dressing."

Recipes for these and other dressings can be found in "Appendix B: The Great Cover-Ups."

ROCK 'N' ROLL CHICKEN

Great grab-and-go food. This recipe can fill a pita or dress up a salad.

$^1/_2$	deli-cooked chicken (remove meat and discard skin)
$^1/_2$ cup	"Sassy Salsa" (see index)
$^1/_2$ cup	sharp Cheddar cheese, shredded
4	flour tortillas (small)

Mix first three ingredients. Put one quarter of the mixture in one tortilla. Roll tightly. (Best to soften tortillas by wetting each under water. Shake dry.) Microwave for one minute.

SPEEDY CHICKEN SALAD SANDWICH

In miniprocessor or food processor, dice one celery stalk and two green onions (cut in chunks). Remove and put in small bowl. Place 1 $^1/_2$ cups of cooked chicken in processor and dice. Add to vegetables and mix in three tablespoons of "Blue Cheese Blast" dressing (see "Appendix B: The Great Cover-Ups"). Serve on bread of choice, over lettuce or rolled up in a tortilla.

8

BAG A BBQ

Brush deli chicken with the following sauce and serve. You can sear it on the BBQ grill or under the broiler for a homemade touch.

WOW-EE! BAR-B-QUE SAUCE

4 tsp.	ketchup (see shortcut below)
2 tsp.	red wine vinegar
2 tsp.	honey
1 tsp.	chili powder
1 tsp.	garlic powder

In a small bowl, mix together the above ingredients. Microwave for one and a half minutes until hot. This blends the flavors. Prepare, then arrange chicken pieces on serving plate. Brush or spoon sauce over chicken and serve.

SHORTCUT

- *Learn to gauge your tablespoon and tea-spoon measurements. Once you know what a half teaspoon **looks** like, you won't need to clean measuring spoons each time.*

DIRTY LITTLE KITCHEN SECRETS

Is your cooking making you or anyone else sick? Maybe it's not your recipes but the hidden "kitchen cooties" that can lurk on your hands, in your blender or on your cutting board. Revealing some very nasty kitchen habits and habitats, our very first guest,* a kitchen sanitation specialist, set us on the straight and narrow path of safe food handling.

PERSONAL HYGIENE
- *Wash hands often and use an antibacterial soap. Hands are potentially the most dangerous item in the kitchen.*
- *Use a tightly woven kitchen towel for cleanup. Rinse and air-dry quickly. Change daily. Sponges are not recommended because they trap food particles and are hard to sanitize.*

FOOD PROCESSOR AND BLENDER
- *Take apart and clean after every use.*
- *Wash parts in dishwasher or use an antibacterial soap.*
- *Rinse well and air-dry, upside down.*
- *Blender gaskets should be replaced yearly or when worn.*

CUTTING BOARD
- *Utilize both sides: one side for raw foods, the other for cooked.*
- *Wash with a bleach sanitizer and rinse in hot water after every use. Air-dry.*
- *Do not let it sit in water.*

FLASH RECIPE

COOTIE B-GONE: 1 Tablespoon bleach per 1 quart of water. Put in clearly labeled spray bottle. Use to disinfect countertops and other surfaces.

* Dan Morrow is Senior Department Director of Food and Nutrition Services at Mt Diablo Medical Center, Concord, California.

FIESTA FIASCO

We love the "canniness" of Mexican food, which is keen on taste and works well in hectic moments.

These recipes are easy to prepare and sure to please. The ingredients in Mexican dishes are a cinch to find in most supermarkets and stock well in your pantry.

We salute — the marvelous musical fruit — the resounding, burly BEAN.

Beans play a major role in Mexican dishes. They are a healthy resource in keeping harmony in the kitchen. Canned beans are cook-friendly: Spread 'em, top 'em, fill 'em or mix 'em. They're ready when you are (and even when you're not).

Beans are pantry-ready: red, black, white, large or small, beans pack a powerful punch for the hurried cook. By providing a variety of flavors, colors and textures, they create delicious and fast fiestas.

SASSY SALSA

*Lisa's three-minute salsa is such a hit, you can call her Lisa**Rita**! Use "Sassy Salsa" as a dip, a base for sauces, a recipe enhancer, or — as a facial mask (just kidding!). Keep it handy. This recipe makes one quart and lasts up to three weeks refrigerated.*

2	**14 ¹/₂-oz. cans stewed tomatoes**
1	**bunch cilantro, wash and remove stems**
¹/₄	**bunch parsley (optional)**
1	**small red onion, peeled**
1¹/₂ Tbs.	**chili powder**
1¹/₂ Tbs.	**garlic powder**
1 tsp.	**cayenne (1-1¹/₂ tsp. "Some like it hot!")**
¹/₂ tsp.	**lemon juice**
¹/₂ tsp.	**sugar (¹/₂-1 tsp. "Some like it sweet!")**

Add stewed tomatoes first, then the cilantro and seasonings to blender. Chop for about 30 seconds, until mixed. Pour into a one-quart glass jar. A clean, recycled mayonnaise jar works well!

SHORTCUTS
- *It's all-in-one and one-for-all: There's no need to chop, dice, etc. Dump ingredients directly into the blender and let **it** do the work.*
- *Save time by using canned tomatoes.*
- *Keep a "plastic lemon" in the refrigerator. It's handy when just a little squirt is needed.*

Side By Side

It was a pot luck — of friends. With Cinco De Mayo not far away, we themed our second show around a fiasco, uhh — fiesta.

Everyone brought a little something from home to decorate the set. The pull-together potluck of items filled the studio with creativity and fun. By the time closing credits came, Brad's (our production assistant's) sombrero had found its way onto John's (a cameraman's) head. With the whole crew following, we danced the "Mexican Hat Dance" in celebration of our second completed production. We finished before midnight!

FOR A LOW-FAT FIESTA

Scott putting the mike on Lisa before taping a show.

Salsa
- Many canned and jarred Mexican salsas contain oil. Save money and fat calories by making your own sauce.
- Choose lite sour cream when dressing tacos, burritos, etc.

Ground Beef
- Look for lean meat products when purchasing. Extra lean, ground sirloin hamburger **should be** very low in fat.

- What you see is not always what you get. Prepackaged hamburger can have a higher fat content then what is stated on the label. To make certain your ground beef is low-fat, ask your butcher to triple grind lean stew meat. This will save fat calories and can cost less per pound than ground sirloin.

Tortillas
- Check out the choices in tortillas: corn, white corn, whole and sprouted-wheat.
- Read the nutrition label. A product may contain hidden fat.
- Avoid lard and cottonseed oil.

MEXZANYA

Terrie's "Mexican Lasagna" and Lisa's "Sassy Salsa"
recipes create a fast and hearty favorite.

1 lb.	extra lean ground beef, cooked (meat optional)
2	lite flour tortillas, large
3.8 oz.	can sliced ripe olives, drained
15 oz.	can corn, drained
30 oz.	can nonfat refried beans
4 oz.	can diced green chiles, drained
8 oz.	sharp Cheddar cheese, shredded
1 Tbs.	garlic powder
1 Tbs.	chili powder
2 cups	"Sassy Salsa" (see page 12)

Use a microwaveable pie dish. Coat bottom with
$1/2$ cup of salsa. Place one tortilla on top of salsa.
Spread on half can of softened beans over tortilla.
Spread half of meat on top of beans. Sprinkle with
half the spices. Continue to add half of corn,
olives, chilies. Pour $1/2$ cup of salsa over mixture.
Add half of cheese. Repeat for a second layer,
ending with the cheese and final $1/2$ cup of salsa.
Loosely cover then microwave for approximately
8 to 10 minutes — until cheese is melted and
contents are hot.

SHORTCUTS

- *Reuse the same containers and utensils throughout the recipe to save cleanup time.*
- *Double the recipe, then freeze half. Can be frozen in a foil pie plate. (Just don't micro-wave in that!) Wrap well.*
- *Cover the bottom of your microwave with paper towels for an easy cleanup.*
- *Briefly heat refried beans, on a paper plate in the microwave, to get them to spread easier.*

CHICKEN CHOWDER PIE

Make your kitchen work for you! This recipe visits the freezer, refrigerator and the pantry to create a favorite family fixin'.

2	tortillas (flour or corn)
3	chicken breasts, cook and grind in miniprocessor
4 oz.	can diced green chilies
1$^{1}/_{2}$ cups	frozen Southwest-type salad* ($^{1}/_{2}$ pkg.), thawed
16 oz.	New England clam chowder (low-fat)
$^{1}/_{2}$ cup	Cheddar cheese, shredded
1 cup	"Sassy Salsa" (see page 12)

Cover bottom of pie plate with one-fourth the salsa. Place one tortilla on it. Layer the following in this order: half the ground chicken, half the chilies, $^{3}/_{4}$ cup frozen salad, half a can of clam chowder. Place another tortilla on top and repeat layers. Sprinkle with cheese. Loosely cover with plastic wrap. Microwave for 15 minutes on high.

SHORTCUTS

- *Purchase prebagged, frozen boneless chicken breasts and keep in your freezer. Defrost just what you need, as you need it, in the microwave.*
- *To cook chicken breast in microwave: Place three chicken breasts on a microwave-able plate and cover with plastic wrap. Cook on high for 6 to 8 minutes. (To check chicken for doneness, pierce with a fork — juices should be clear.) Cut into chunks and grind in miniprocessor.*

*This type of salad product contains sweet corn, black beans, red and green peppers plus celery. Keep this freezer-ready for instant color and taste. For a quick thaw, place frozen salad in a colander under cold running water.

TO BEAN OR NOT TO BEAN? . . .

. . . That is the question.

Beans are such a healthy food. With complex carbohydrates and proteins they're a sure-fire winner. But, they can backfire. Tummies can rumble and friends leave suddenly without saying good-bye. Here's how to put the beans back into your life and still have friends.

Our fiesta guest* was a gastroenterologist specializing in heartburn. He was a bit more graphic than anticipated. So, here are the details (minus the graphics).

HEARTBURN

Heartburn, which has nothing to do with the heart, is caused when stomach acid flows backward into the esophagus.

Lifestyle Tips

1. *Eat small meals; this produces less pressure in your stomach.*
2. *Eat slowly; eating in a hurry can overwhelm your stomach.*
3. *Eat early. It takes about three hours for your stomach to empty.*
4. *Oily, fatty and fried foods stay in your stomach longer.*
5. *Spicy foods, acidic foods, chocolate and peppermint may bring on symptoms.*
6. *Caffeine, smoking and alcohol can also be culprits.*

- *If you have heartburn at bedtime, raise your upper body by 6 to 8 inches. Use a foam rubber wedge under your head and shoulders.*
- *There are medications. If heartburn **persists**, see your doctor or pharmacist.*

GAS

Gas is caused mainly by dietary fiber. Fiber is good but for many it can have undesirable effects, like sleeping alone!

- *By increasing the amount of fiber **slowly** in your diet, your system will be able to adjust, therefore producing less gas.*
- *There are over-the-counter products to take before a meal that reduce the symptoms. (We've been known to spike our husbands' food.)*

* *Mervyn D. Becker, M.D., Gastroenterologist, Concord, California.*

PEOPLE-PLEASIN' PICNICS

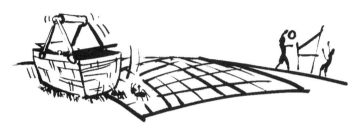

These shop-n-plop recipes are so easy! They are designed for that spur of the moment, by-the-seat-of-your-pants picnic. Pssst! Bring your can opener !

Begin at the deli section of your supermarket. Buy your favorite meat and have it freshly sliced. Check the meat for marbling: Less marbling equals less fat content. Also, be aware that cold cuts usually are high in sodium.

Some of our favorite choices:
- *98% fat-free, oven-roasted turkey breast or Bar-B-Q turkey.*
- *Low-fat ham: honey-glazed, Black Forest or Virginia baked.*
- *From the supermarket's fresh salad bar, select the necessary odds and ends like lettuce, sliced tomatoes, sliced onions, napkins, knives, spoons, etc.*

SUPER CHICKEN HERO

Here's an on-the-spot sandwich.

1 lb.	loaf sweet French bread
$^3/_4$ lb.	chicken breast (or your choice), sliced
1	tomato, sliced thin
1	red onion, sliced thin
7 oz.	jar roasted red peppers, drained
6 oz.	jar sharp Cheddar cheese spread

Slice loaf lengthwise. Spread cheese on both top and bottom. Arrange meat slices, tomatoes, onions and peppers on bottom of bread. Place top on bread to make large sandwich. Cut into 3" portions.

SHORTCUT
* *Try selecting already cleaned and sliced items from the salad bar.*

Side Show

*To add another dimension to "The ShortCut Cook," we decided to go **on location**, and tape Lisa in a supermarket reviewing some favorite food products.*

*So, before our scheduled studio production, we went to Diablo Foods, Lafayette, California, with high hopes and **no** experience. Our faithful and patient camera operator, John Murray, shot the segments and Terrie's husband Scott directed — foot traffic.*

Inspired by the rows and rows of edibles, Lisa was on a roll. We got our first real peek at Lisa's love affair with food. We should have called these segments: "Fantasy Aisleland."

It was also the viewers' first peek at Terrie's new granddaughter, Kendra. We started to sneak her into inconspicuous background shots and she became our famous "Whose baby is that?" mascot.

On the Side

Getting ANOTHER itch to broaden our creativity (and see how much we could cram into one day), we pulled out all the stops. Actually we pulled out the Hi-8 video camera. Thus, we incorporated our homelife into the show.

Taping in Terrie's kitchen, we produced "Cookin' Cupboards," what foods the everyday cook should keep on hand — from the pantry to the freezer.

Our family and dining rooms provided the right atmosphere for clips of our own "guinea pigs" (family members) braving the waters before you do. We officially refer to them as our "ShortCut Taste Testers." It was so cute: our husbands molded to their recliners, giving us culinary opinions — then asking for seconds!

TORTILLA ROLL-UPS

Cheaper by the dozen! (Tortillas also make a great substitute for the expensive Lavosh bread.) You can make this roll-up sandwich a day in advance. Refrigerate. It keeps for 24 hours.

2	**lite flour tortillas**
8 oz.	**tub lite cream cheese**
1/2 lb.	**turkey breast (or deli meat of choice)**
1	**tomato, thinly sliced**
4	**leaves of lettuce**
4	**thin slices of onion**

To soften each tortilla, wet lightly with water and shake off excess. Place tortilla on paper plate. Spread each with some cream cheese. Layer half of meat, tomato, lettuce and onion on each tortilla. Roll tightly and cover with plastic wrap. Refrigerate. When ready to serve, slice into two-inch rounds.

SHORTCUT
- *For a really fast start, pick up cleaned and sliced ingredients at a salad bar.*

ARTICHOKE AND BEAN SALAD

A toss-and-serve favorite. The artichoke hearts add lots of interest.

15 oz.	jar/can marinated bean salad (kidney, garbanzo, green), drained
6 oz.	jar marinated artichoke hearts, drained
6 oz.	jar mushrooms, drained (optional)

Add all the above to a resealable plastic bag, or a clean recycled produce bag. Shake and serve!

PEACH ANGEL CAKE

You have to try this. Fresh, frozen or canned — experiment with your favorite fruit. It's unbelievably fast, easy, low-fat and delicious.

1	large angel food cake (store-bought)
15 oz.	can lite peaches, drain (then cut into smaller pieces while still in the can)
2	8-oz. containers nonfat peach yogurt

Slice cake crosswise. Spread with a third of the yogurt and peaches. Replace the top of the cake. Cover with remaining yogurt and peaches.

Outside

Back at our kitchenless studio, Brad, our graphic and set designer, did magic today. With a frisbee, butterfly net, folding chairs, even a fly swatter (each show seems to have a scheduled appearance for a fly), he transformed our humble kitchen "resemblance" into a backyard! And the rest was a picnic.

FROM THE FREEZER

- *Three easy steps to a quick **fruit salad**. Pick up a bag of frozen mixed fruit. It will stay cold and help keep other picnic items cool. When you get to the park, open and drain off excess fruit juice. Mix the following right into the bag:*

    1) *sliced fresh banana*
    2) *small package of chopped nuts*
    3) *8-oz. container of your favorite yogurt*

Brad usually helps before the cameras start to roll (with set-up and set design). Here he fills in during a live shoot.

JUST DOING IT

This was a "just do it" segment. We know how hard it is to get time away. So, using our natural resources, we invited a Regional Park District representative* to map out locations and ideas for an inexpensive minivacation. Here are tips on:

CHOOSING YOUR LOCATION

Take Advantage of the Regional Parks in Your Area, even if it's only for a quick family meal. There are many hidden treasures in your area you probably don't know about.

Choose your Park to Suit your Activity. Do you want to: hike, fish, star gaze, sail, horseback ride, spend the night, relax and just do nothing . . . or go all-out and do it all?

Give the Park District a Call, for Some Brochures. Remember; Your tax dollars made it all possible — you might as well enjoy it.

KEEPING YOUR FOOD SAFE

Take the necessary precautions to keep food safe to eat. Cold foods should remain cold. Invest in a reliable cooler and bring plenty of ice.

Keep your own cooler ice handy by filling recycled milk cartons and empty liter bottles with water and storing them in your freezer.

Picnic baskets are romantic and fun — but you must use caution when dealing with food. Don't leave food out in the heat.

Some susceptible foods:
- *Foods containing egg*
- *Foods containing mayonnaise*
- *Meats*
- *Milk products*

FOLLOWING THE RULES

Be Aware of Park Restrictions Concerning Alcohol.

No hard liquor is allowed; some parks allow beer and wine only for large reserved groups. Check with the park beforehand.

Remember: Don't drink and swim. Only fish can do that!

* Mark Ragatz, Reservations Supervisor, East Bay Regional Park District, Oakland, California.

FASTA' PASTA

*Through thick or thin, the long and short of it is — pasta can save you **time** and money. It is an absolute **must** for every pantry. It's so versatile you can make it year round and use it in soups, salads and main dishes. It cooks up in no time and is great for extending leftovers to feed extra guests. It always seems to taste better the next day, and the next, and so on.*

Pasta comes in dozens of interesting shapes, sizes and thickness. Variety performs real functions; like "holding" a sauce, adding texture, dimension and visual appeal. (A friend of ours actually has a pasta museum.)

Look for "100% Durum Semolina" — made with only flour and water — no fat. Imported pastas are noted for being rich in flavor and texture.

AUNTIE DOLLY'S CECI (chĕ´ chē) PASTA

This ten-minute pasta dish gives Italian ceci beans (garbanzos) a new flavor.

$^1/_2$ lb.	cooked semolina pasta (spaghetti)
14 oz.	can garbanzo beans (do not drain)
11 oz.	can Italian tomato soup
1 Tbs.	Italian herb seasonings
2 Tbs.	garlic powder
1	can stewed tomatoes (cut into small pieces while still in the can)
8 oz.	pkg. frozen, assorted sliced peppers, thawed (optional)
$^1/_2$ tsp.	crushed red pepper flakes
$^1/_4$ cup	Parmesan cheese

Cook and drain pasta and put back in pot. Add the beans with liquid, $^1/_2$ can soup and all the remaining ingredients. (Peppers really add a lot of color. You'll need about one cup.) Mix and serve hot right from the pot. Parmesan cheese and crushed red peppers finish the dish.

SHORTCUT
- *Use vermicelli. It cooks up in under four minutes. Or use the extra, frozen pasta you cooked up last month.*

Side Effects

*It was two for the price of one. This was the first night we taped two shows in **one** evening. Our guests arrived early and we were running late. The "Terrible Twos" are in double the trouble.*

Our second show of the evening finds us scrambling to remake our backyard set into an Italian restaurant. We trade a picnic scene for a pasta fling and "mamma mia," the heat is on! Large, uncooked strands of pasta replace the butterfly net and miniature Italian flags and a checkerboard tablecloth are now where our frisbee was.

It's very late. Taping two shows with too little time makes for a cranky crew. Lisa's energy was fading like Terrie's confidence. There was murmuring in the camp. We were really learning how to live a life full of creative alternatives; making do with what you have (letting go of everything else), just like pantry-ready cooking.

Lots of "letting go" this night — first the schedule; then a little patience; next was pride; the rest was sleep.

NO FEAR ALFREDO

Tastes too good. It must be fattening. Well, have no fear — "No Fear Alfredo's" here! Loads of flavor with very little fat.

¹/₂ lb.	cooked semolina pasta (fettuccine)
8 oz.	lite sour cream
6 oz.	lite cream cheese
1¹/₂ Tbs.	sugar
¹/₂ tsp.	nutmeg
¹/₄ cup	Parmesan cheese

Cook pasta. Drain. Remove pasta. To the pot, add all the above. Heat until blended. Pour fettuccine back into pot. Mix and serve hot.

TASTE TIP
- Lite sour cream and lite cream cheese products have more flavor than bland nonfat varieties. You might as well "go for it." Enjoy the rich taste. Although the fats differ, total calorie cost is nearly **equal**.

PASSION PASTA

Is it the flavor, or because it is so easy to make, that you're — in love?

1 lb.	cooked spaghetti
16 oz.	can soup, fat free clam chowder
15 oz.	stewed tomatoes, chopped and drained
4 oz.	can sliced mushrooms, drained
$1/2$ cup	sherry
8 oz.	lite sour cream
2 Tbs.	garlic powder
1 lb.	bay shrimp, precooked
$1^1/_2$ lb.	imitation crab

In a blender, puree clam chowder and tomatoes. This makes the base for your pasta sauce. In medium pot, add sliced mushrooms, wine, sour cream and garlic powder. Add soup, stir. Add shrimp and crab to hot pasta sauce 3 minutes before serving. Serve over pasta. Sprinkle with Parmesan.

RAVING RAVIOLI

14 oz.	box frozen cheese ravioli (cooked)
10 oz.	can Italian tomato soup
$^1/_4$ cup	white wine
$^1/_2$ cup	Parmesan cheese
1 tsp.	red pepper flakes

Pour soup into nonstick saucepan. Heat until warm. Add wine, stir over medium heat for 2 minutes. Place drained ravioli on platter and top with the heated sauce. Sprinkle with cheese and red pepper flakes. So E A S Y, the kids can help with this.

ITALIAN CLAM PASTA

2	$10^1/_4$-oz. cans soup, low-fat clam chowder
14 oz.	can Italian stewed tomatoes, drained
4 oz.	lite sour cream
2 Tbs.	Worcestershire sauce
2 Tbs.	garlic powder

In a blender, puree soup with tomatoes. In a large bowl, mix sour cream with seasonings, then add soup mixture. Microwave until heated through and serve over your favorite pasta.

TEN-MINUTE PASTA SAUCE

2	15-oz. cans stewed tomatoes
8 oz.	tomato sauce
8 oz.	package fresh mushrooms, sliced
2 Tbs.	Italian dried herbs
2 Tbs.	garlic powder
1 Tbs.	browning and seasoning sauce

Heat all the above in a medium, nonstick saucepan until hot. (Or, microwave in a bowl about 6 minutes on high.) Serve with hot pasta.

FIVE-MINUTE PASTA SAUCE

$1/2$ lb.	vermicelli, cooked
14 oz.	can tomato bisque soup
1 $1/2$ cup	lite sour cream
2 Tbs.	garlic powder
	Parmesan cheese, to taste
	fresh parsley, minced

In a microwaveable bowl, mix soup with sour cream and garlic. Microwave 2 to 3 minutes on high. Serve over hot pasta. Garnish with Parmesan cheese and fresh parsley.

B.Y.O. . . S!

(Bring Your Own . . . Stove!)

This celebrity guest* was a great catch for "The ShortCut Cook." As a cookbook author, restaurateur and television chef, this noodle know-it-all enriched our show with his perfect pasta principles.

He must have had his share of doubts when we began to brief him. We had to make it clear that "The ShortCut Cook" was not the typical cooking show. In order to **actually cook** he would have to bring a stove and do without running water. We proposed that he think of it as — a "Gourmet

Gastronome Goes **Camping**!" segment. We could provide a small kettle, a small bucket of water and a small studio.

Being the curious and adventurous type, he agreed to appear. He'll probably never forget this experience, just as we will never forget the look on his face when he saw our so-called kitchen.

* *Carlo Middione, author, instructor, chef/owner of San Francisco's Vivande Porta Via and Vivande Ristorante.*

COOKING TIPS FOR PERFECT PASTA

- Use a large pot (larger than what you might think you'll need) to boil your pasta.

- You have to have pasta cooked 'al dente' (to the tooth). It needs to have some **bite**. Chewing is very good for your digestion because it makes more saliva, helps you digest and feel better.

- Always draw fresh, cold water to start.

- Add one teaspoon of salt for every quart of water (optional).

- Have the water at a rapid boil before adding the pasta.

- Stir the pot after adding pasta. Keep it moving. Don't allow it to glue-up at the bottom of the pot.

- NEVER add oil (not even olive oil). It coats the pasta and causes the sauce to slide off. If you cook pasta correctly (not too done) and stir it often, it won't stick together. Likewise, don't rinse it — just drain it.

- Watch out for a package's cooking directions: "cook until done" . . . "cook 20 minutes." Following this could result in MUSH. Watch your pasta and judge for yourself!

NO-HOST PARTY

You CAN have a party — and enjoy it too! With a little planning, some fast make-ahead recipes and the right guest list, you can be the hassle-free host. You won't get crabby preparing this. These recipes serve six to eight.

"WHAT A CRAB" SPREAD

Sound familiar? Turn imitation crab into a gourmet spread. You and your guests will smile when you taste this no-frown answer to appetizers.

$1/2$ lb.	imitation crab meat, chopped
6 oz.	lite sour cream
$2/3$ cup	sliced almonds
1 Tbs.	garlic powder
$1/2$ tsp.	creamy horseradish
$1/2$ tsp.	sugar

Mix all ingredients. Add only one-half the almonds. Can be made the day before. You can serve it hot or cold. To serve hot, microwave for $1 1/2$ minutes. Top with remaining nuts.

Party Tip: Great topper for crackers or bagel chips. Excellent spread for sliced sourdough baguettes.

GARLIC GETAWAY

8 oz.	pkg. lite cream cheese
$1/2$ cup	sharp Cheddar cheese, shredded
4 oz.	can sliced ripe olives, drained
4 oz.	can diced green chiles, drained
2 Tbs.	garlic powder
1 tsp.	Worcestershire sauce

Place cream cheese on paper plate and microwave 30 seconds to soften. In medium bowl, mix all ingredients well, including cream cheese. Heat on high for 2 to 3 minutes or until cheese melts. Refrigerate, if you have any leftover!

Party Tip: Use as a sandwich spread, dip for veggies or serve on crackers.

VEGETABLES ON PARADE

Make a little fun for you and your guests. Use "old" vegetables you don't want to cook. Or, if on display a short time, just disassemble and cook the next day — especially the cauliflower. Don't worry about it having "set out."

PALM TREE ISLAND

1	head of cauliflower
2	carrots
1	green bell pepper

Wooden skewers
Paring knife
Coordination!

Side Step

The day before we were set to tape, our "celebrity" guest calls and cancels his appearance, promising to appear at another time. Who'd - a-guessed? We had met, scheduled, scripted and confirmed. Then we reconfirmed and faxed, then phoned again. Who'd-a-thought?

Oh, well. Like always, we're gonna make do with what we got. And today we got a new director, Charly!

Actually, he was our director in a previous production for two-and-a-half years. He is very familiar with

Charly and Terrie hang out in the control room.

the old studio equipment — and us old broads. He's also very funny. Just what the "production doctor" would have ordered — if we had one.

- *Trim off the top and bottom of a carrot so it's nice and flat.*
- *Cut small wedges along the "trunk."*

*Here's the **tricky part**:*

- *Take a green pepper and make small 'V' cuts that zigzag around the equator, ending where you started. Pull apart the sections.*
- *Attach pepper "palms" using a small section of wood skewer. Use the pointed end to poke into the carrot; blunt ends, into the pepper and cauliflower. Be careful cutting and poking. Don't confuse your fingers for the carrot!*
- *Now secure the "palm tree" trunks atop the cauliflower "island" using more skewers.*

If that worked, make another palm tree. You're doing better than we did!

If you passed that test, you may want to make a flower that you just can't "beet."

ONION FLOWER
1   onion (or more)
          beet juice (from can or jar product)

Paring knife
Small bowl to hold juice

- *Take one large, white onion. Peel and clean.*
- *Trim root end to make a flat base.*
- *Place upright and make (parallel) vertical cuts* **almost** *to the base.*
- *Turn one quarter and cut across those rows (like you're getting ready to shortcut dice it).*
- *Press the flower open (a bit) and dip it into the beet juice. (Be careful of this part. Don't spill; beet juice* **stains**.)

(What is the magic trick for not crying when cutting onions? For some people nothing works. For Lisa, wearing contacts helps!)

Wayside

Paradise Lost?
It's an island, it's a alien. No, it's a frantic attempt to cover for a no-show guest! Lisa is spearing carrots (and herself), carving green peppers and "planting" them into an unsteady cauliflower island (see "Vegetables on Parade," page 36). She (kind of) observed how to create this vegetable centerpiece on a cruise.

It was a total disaster: a 9.0 on the Richter Scale. What was salvageable? Footage for bloopers and bleepers!

TUNA DIVINE

Transform an everyday canned good into a luxury liner.

2	6-oz. cans water-packed albacore tuna
10 oz.	can low-fat cream of mushroom soup
4 oz.	jar pimientos
4 oz.	sliced almonds
$^1/_2$ cup	Italian bread crumbs
$^1/_4$ cup	Parmesan cheese

In a medium microwaveable bowl, mix all the above. Heat 2 to 3 minutes or until hot.

Party (of one) Tip: For a sandwich, pile this into a pita pocket. Add lettuce and tomato.

SÍ, SÍ OLÉ! (translates: Dip your Chip!)

Fat-free beans and canned green chiles give this dip a "craving" review. Better be prepared. Make two batches — they're going to ask for more.

14 oz.	can fat-free chile beans, drained
8 oz.	lite cream cheese
4 oz.	can diced mild green chiles, drained
4 oz.	can sliced ripe olives, drained
5	green onions, sliced very thin (topping)
	tortilla chips

Mix first four ingredients in a medium microwaveable bowl. Heat 2 minutes on high. Sprinkle with green onions. Serve with your favorite dipping chips.

DANCING SHRIMP COCKTAIL
Ready in less than a minute — fast footwork!

1/2 lb.	bay shrimp
8 oz.	lite cream cheese
4 oz.	bottled chili sauce
	crackers

Place unwrapped block of cream cheese on a decorative medium dish. Spread the cocktail sauce to cover top of cheese. Top with drained shrimp. Place favorite crackers around.

Provide at least two butter knives for guests to scoop "cocktail" onto crackers.

THREE-MINUTE MUSHROOMS

From fresh, to pop-in-your-mouth delicacies, your in-the-cupboard food livens up a party. Make plenty. One batch never seems enough.

1 lb.	whole fresh mushrooms (cleaned)
$1/2$ cup	Italian bread crumbs
2 Tbs.	garlic powder
$1/4$ cup	Parmesan cheese
2 Tbs.	olive oil
2 Tbs.	water

Remove mushroom stems and dice them in miniprocessor. Add the remaining ingredients and mix well. Salt each mushroom cap lightly. Fill with one tablespoon of mixture. Bake on cookie sheet at 400° for 10 minutes. Test ONE to make sure they are not **too** hot to serve. OK, test TWO. (Just don't eat the whole bunch!)

SHORTCUTS
- *Cover cookie sheet with foil for easy cleanup (recycle this where you can).*
- *Make in advance. Then place on microwave-able serving plate and heat for 2 minutes or until hot.*

HAWAIIAN HAM BITES

These tiny morsels of sweetness taste really good! A healthy alternative to the ever-present peanut dish. Make in an instant. You need go no farther than your pantry or fridge to assemble these goodies.

¹/₂ lb.	**extra lean ham, thinly sliced**
4 oz.	**can pineapple chunks, drained**
	fancy toothpicks

Take one slice of ham and place one piece of pineapple in center. (If the slices are large, cut in half.) Roll ham around pineapple and secure with toothpick.

IT'S MY PARTY AND I'LL SIT IF I WANT TO . . .

FOR EASY MENU PLANNING

- *KISS: Keep It Short and Simple. This mind-set will help focus your time and energy on **enjoying**!*
- *Finger foods are perfect: Less fuss, less mess = less cleanup.*
- *Select a recipe that can be made days before and freeze if need be.*
- *Select recipes that taste better after a few days — like lasagna.*
- *Store rice, soups, etc., in resealable plastic bags. Food won't take up as much room and the smaller quantities enable fast reheating and replenishing. When the party is over, simply freeze unused bags for another day.*
- *Reheat (microwave) right in the bag (vent first). No extra bowls to wash.*
- *Have "fillers," like pasta, bread or rolls, potato dishes, or stuffed crepes. (Some people eat like it's their "last supper.")*
- *Invite a few gourmet show-offs who always insist on bringing something (then let them)!*

FOR MORE FUN SERVING

- *Set a pretty buffet table and make guests **want** to serve themselves.*
- *Invite a few workaholics.*

FOR FAST CLEANUP

- *Spray all cookware with nonstick coating for easy washing.*
- *Use paper plates. For a more formal look, buy decorated ones!*
- *Place garbage bags in obvious places. (Every so often, openly demonstrate their function.)*
- *Invite your mother.*

LOW-FAT SNACK ATTACK

Snacking has become our easiest way to consume a meal. We are producing the show and **developing** *recipes, working our day jobs and* **testing** *recipes. We're on a roll (and eating 'em too) with interviews, paperwork — and developing and* **tasting** *MORE recipes.*

By the time dinner comes, we're full. By the time production day comes — we've gained another five pounds. At this rate, by next year, we'll need elevators installed, ". . .'cause no way, no how — we're going to make it up those stairs!"

CLAM KICK DIP

Dip into this "sea-licious," kick-start spread for a real fast snack-in-a-snap.

2	6 $^1/_2$-oz. cans minced clams, drained
8 oz.	lite cream cheese
2 Tbs.	Worcestershire sauce
2 $^1/_2$ Tbs.	garlic powder
$^1/_2$	medium white onion, diced
$^1/_2$ tsp.	salt

Mix all the above and spread on your favorite cracker or veggie.

John (camera) and Scott (audio) exchange pleasantries between takes.

TORTILLA FILLER-UPPER

Here's how to make a snack right out of your cupboard and fridge. This is something you can eat for breakfast, lunch or dinner.

2	low-fat flour tortillas
2 Tbs.	lite cream cheese
1/4 lb.	lean, deli sliced ham
1/4 cup	low-fat mozzarella cheese
6	pepperoncinis

Spread tortilla with cream cheese, ham, pepperoncinis and half the mozzarella. Top with second tortilla and sprinkle with remaining mozzarella. Heat in microwave for 1 minute, or until cheese melts. Slice into quarters.

SHORTCUT
* *Use a pizza cutter to "roll right through" tortillas or pita bread.*

SPROUTED-WHEAT TORTILLA PIZZA

Here's another fast way to utilize the handy tortilla.

4	sprouted whole-wheat tortillas (or large corn tortillas)
10 1/2 oz.	can Italian tomato soup
4 oz.	can mushrooms, drained
1/4 lb.	Monterey Jack cheese, sliced
2 tsp.	garlic pepper
	Parmesan cheese to taste

Spread two tablespoons of undiluted soup directly on tortilla to cover. Layer on half the cheese, mushrooms and garlic pepper. Cover with second tortilla. Spread top with two more tablespoons of soup and the remainders of cheese, mushrooms and pepper. Sprinkle with Parmesan. Place on microwaveable plate and cook on high for one minute. Or bake in oven at 450° for 5 minutes — just until cheese melts. (Save leftover soup for a small pasta dinner or freeze for later use in another soup or sauce.)

Be-Side Ourselves

Having a last minute, no-show guest found Lisa and Terrie grasping for an idea for the show's interview segment.

"Terrie — I got it! Let's both make our own bouquet arrangement from fruits and vegetables. It's easy, I saw this demonstrated on a cruise."
"Are you CRAZY? Do you think I'm crazy? You're gonna die out there — and take me with you."

"It's so easy. You just select what vegetable, fruits and flowers you want to use from the tray in front.

Skewer and place it in the jar. Don't worry. I'll talk you through it."

So for fifteen "skewering" minutes, Lisa talked and talked, and Terrie took and took. (Took advantage and took all the flowers while Lisa's hands were busy "talking.")

If you really want to learn how to make this kind of veggie display, we suggest you go on a cruise. It's a lot more fun!

SNACKING KNOW-HOW*

You Can Snack and Not Get Fat, But Keep in Mind:

- It's about eating small, frequent meals and eating light at night. Eat when you are hungry and stop when you're comfortably full. You will be hungry usually two to three hours later. That's a good pattern to get into. That way you are eating small meals and never over-eating — nibbling vs. gorging.

- You will probably eat MORE calories eating a fat-reduced product if it doesn't have that satisfying taste.

- As you age, every calorie counts. Your need for calories decreases as you age but your need for certain vitamins and minerals increases! The average person has increased his daily intake, by more than 200 calories, over that of previous years. Even low and no-fat foods have calories and can make you fat if you eat **too** much!

- If cookies and candies are too irresistible, give yourself just a couple. If you give yourself what you crave at the times when you crave it, you have a better chance of not overeating those things.

* From Elaine Magee, R.D., author, columnist.

PLEASE DON'T EAT THE DAISIES

To be very blunt, this portion has nothing to do with low-fat snacks. Our scheduled guest didn't show up and we needed to come up with something — really quick.

Lisa had just returned from a cruise where she had watched someone demonstrate how to make a vegetable centerpiece. We happened to have all the right ingredients: some leftover produce, studio flowers and a desperate need to fill fifteen very long minutes.

- *Start with a mason jar and fill with water. Use asparagus to give height to your arrangement (tall things can be 1^1/$_2$ times the height of the container). Dill and rosemary sprigs make good filler for the greenery.*
- *Spear vegetables on bamboo skewers for extra height. (Be careful here; poke **away** from your fingers.)*
- *Add things like small boiling onions, cherry tomatoes or red grapes to give contrast and color. Include fresh or silk flowers to really show off.*
- *Open a brown paper lunch bag and lower the jar into it. If the bag is too tall, roll a "cuff" from the top edge.*
- *Gather the bag around the neck of the jar and tie with a bright ribbon (or kitchen twine for a country look).*

FIRE-CRACKIN' SALADS

*Celebrate Independence Day by **not** toiling in the kitchen. Show a little salad savvy. Buy cleaned lettuce or baby spinach in a bag and keep ready-made salad dressing in the fridge. Heck, you can even find jarred bacon pieces in a low-fat version so that you can save time **and** calories.*

Get a bang out of your salads by adding freshly cut herbs such as cilantro, parsley, watercress, tarragon, thyme and basil. Caution, it's a flavor explosion! Rocket your way to FIVE-A-DAY — just add frozen fruit and vegetables. They give bursts of flavor, color and texture to the meekest of salads. Be sure to store your favorites.

*These hearty, make-and-take salads are meant to free up your time for some **fun**. Do it your way — today.*

TURKEY ALMOND TOSS

This main dish is a treat that beats the heat!

1 lb.	pkg. precooked turkey breast
4 oz.	pkg. sliced almonds
4 oz.	can sliced water chestnuts
1/2 cup	celery, chopped
1/2 cup	green onions, diced
1/2 cup	low-fat mayonnaise

Have the butcher cube the meat and ask that the skin be removed first. This makes it a snap to prepare. In a medium bowl, add ingredients. Toss. Serve on a bed of lettuce.

SHRIMPLY MARVELOUS SALAD

This is substantial and easy to assemble. It's a festive hit for parties. Make it the day before.

1 lb.	fresh bay shrimp
1 cup	crispy chow mein noodles
1/2 cup	green onions, diced
1/2 cup	low-fat mayonnaise
1/2 cup	celery, diced

Mix all the above ingredients. Refrigerate. If you prefer crispy noodles, add right before serving.

Side Piece

After months of being the "begging babes," Terrie and Lisa connected with a cabinet shop that graciously transformed the homemade set into a look-alike, pull-apart kitchen.

Brad, our graphic designer (and artist-in-tow), put his pencil to paper and by the next month — voilà! Our seven-foot-high, four-piece, modular kitchen adorned the 10' x 16' studio.

CORNY SALAD

Use this salad as a relish or a side dish. It is naturally low in fat and is great year round.

1	10 $^1/_2$-oz. can kernel corn, drained
3 Tbs.	sweet pickle relish
2 Tbs.	lite mayonnaise
1 Tbs.	sweet hot mustard
1 Tbs.	chopped pimiento, optional

Combine all ingredients in a bowl and mix well. Serve as relish or on a bed of lettuce.

FLASH RECIPE

MIXED BAG SALAD

1 bag	prepackaged lettuce (your choice)
$^1/_4$ cup	cilantro, chopped
11 oz.	can mandarin oranges, drained
1	avocado, chopped
1	large tomato, chopped

- *Bottled dressing suggestion: any red wine, vinegar-based, herb blend.*
- *Sprinkle with sliced almonds, toasted lightly (optional).*

The studio never looked so small, the ceiling so low or the stairs so steep. Then again — we had never looked so good!

Our art wizard, Brad, hard at work on the plans for our kitchen set.

LEAN, GREEN AND ALREADY CLEAN!

Rows and rows of bagged, ready-to-use salad greens line your market's produce shelves. Utilize these favorite quickies for an instant salad.

Find: Spring Mix, Baby Spinach, Butter Lettuce (our favorite), Romaine, Red Leaf and specialty greens like Endive, Escarole, Radicchio and many mixed combinations (some with dressings and croutons right in the package).

Remember: Convenience comes with a price. (If you have more time than money, buy the head lettuces — and bag your own.) To get the most for your money, choose firm, fresh leaves. The edges or tips shouldn't be brown. Soft varieties, like Butter Lettuce and Red Leaf, should be flexible but not limp, while crisp counterparts, like Romaine, should be "crackin' crisp." The greener (dark green) the lettuce — the more vitamins it contains.

KITCHEN HELP AT YOUR FINGERTIPS!

We're so jazzed about our new studio kitchen, we decided that today's special guest* had to be the man of our dreams — the one who makes all our DREAM KITCHENS come true.

We asked this expert craftsman to demonstrate some handy cupboard gizmos found in the ultimate kitchen, designs that make kitchen work fun and entertaining an ease.

WALK-IN (and around) PANTRY
Shelves that slide, and racks that roll. The pantry resembles a 21st-century minimart (almost as big as our studio). The kitchen: If it's loaded, you mu$t be!

MOVE-OVER CUPBOARDS
*   A swing-away spice rack behind a cupboard door, allows access from both sides, plus storage behind.
*   A gliding pegboard that stows behind a cabinet door to house lots of utensils and saucepans.
*   Pull-out shelves that help you get to those hard-to-reach items in back. Great for deep cupboards!

* *Steve Rossi, owner, El Monte Cabinets, Concord, California.*

TREASURED ISLAND

Kitchen islands are multifunctional and a paradise for cooks. If you have a wall, you may be able to create an island space — especially if it adjoins a family room. It will add openness and make a kitchen more welcoming.
Its design enables you to:
*   Store with accessibility from all sides.
*   Prepare meals easily with extra counter space.
*   Dine comfortably with extra seating.

APPLIANCE ELEVATORS

It's not really an elevator. It is a movable shelf that your appliance rides on. It pulls out and up to countertop level, without a lot of effort. This is practical and can save you money because now you might just use that Incredible Mango Masher more often. (MUSAK is optional.)

COUNTERTOPS

Corian* is noted for its easy upkeep but pricy selections. It is a great all-purpose work surface with lots of decorative choices. Its smooth surface makes cleanup easy. Corian can scratch, stain or burn but these are a cinch to remove.

*We are proud to say that "The ShortCut Cook" set is equipped with Corian — a cutting board!

BUILDING OR REMODELING YOUR KITCHEN?

Keep in mind the Triangular Work Pattern: Place the sink, stove and refrigerator (major work areas of the kitchen) in a triangle pattern for efficiency. Set them apart from conflicting normal, daily foot traffic.

LOVEABLE VEGETABLES

Hide and seek, the fun game that all ages play. For example, "take my vegetables — please!"

Our children hide them and, sometimes, we find them. As cooks we try to disguise them but kids always seem to identify them.

For us it's in the sauce or under the potatoes. For them, it's under the cushion or in the dog. The game goes on — five servings a day!

Master these dishes and create recipes that make vegetables lovable, uhh . . . likable. Oh, all right — edible.

We take the bold, 90's approach. Be upfront, be who you are — and be good. Eat your veggies!

The following vegetable recipes:
1) Have been taste tested (it's a crew requirement).
2) Our kids will eat!

BROCCOLI BLOW-OUT

This veggie will get gobbled down with this low-fat sauce to dress it up!

1 lb.	or bunch fresh broccoli flowerets, cut in bite-size pieces
3 oz.	jar of low-fat bacon pieces
4 oz.	can sliced water chestnuts, drained
3/4 cup	sliced almonds

CROSS DRESSING: Use hot or cold.

Mix the following:

1 cup	low-fat mayonnaise
1/4 cup	sugar
3 Tbs.	red wine vinegar
1 tsp.	curry powder

Add dressing to broccoli, bacon, water chestnuts and almonds. Mix and serve.

Here is one way to eat your vegetables — with lots of flavor! This recipe can be cooked as well. Microwave for 6 minutes on high.

Side Tracked

Lisa is destroying the new kitchen! There's shrimp on the floor, wantons stuck to the faucet and ham in her hair. It's a real food fight and the food's winning.

"Where's the cream cheese?" she asks ON THE AIR! "Terrie, you forgot to buy the cream cheese."

"No, I put it on the tray in front of you . . . somewhere . . . "

"I don't see a tray."

SHORTCUTS

- *Broccoli is always available. It is usually inexpensive for the good nutritional value it gives but it should come with a warning label. Being a high-fiber green, it's one of the gassier vegetables. It's nutritious raw but easier to digest when cooked.*
- *Use flowerets in salads, there's less waste.*
- *Buy by the bunch, not by the pound when purchasing whole, stem-on broccoli.*
- *You can use the stalk if you peel it first.*

SAUCED SPINACH

2	10-oz. pkgs. frozen creamed spinach (97% fat free), drain
3 oz.	low-fat bacon pieces
$1/2$ cup	chopped frozen onions, thawed
$1/4$ cup	Italian bread crumbs.

Thaw spinach in package. Add all the above to a medium microwaveable bowl. Microwave on high for 2 minutes. It's ready to serve!

Nobody could. The counter looks like a recycling bin. Empty cans, open bottles and paper boxes are blocking EVERYONE'S view. Never again will we do six recipes in less than 12 minutes!

Robyn's help proved to be a real life-saver many times.

59

SOME SPICY CARROTS

Using fancy round carrots is another way to eat more vegetables. They're tasty, convenient and a "shmancy" way to get your FIVE-A-DAY.

16 oz.	package frozen sliced carrots (or vegetable mixtures), thaw, drain
1 cup	white sweet onion, chopped
1 cup	green pepper, chopped

VEGGIE MARINADE

8 oz.	tomato sauce
1/4 cup	vinegar
1/4 cup	olive oil
1 Tbs.	sugar
1 tsp.	dry mustard, or 1 Tbs. sweet hot mustard
1 tsp.	Worcestershire sauce

Combine all ingredients in a bowl. Add thawed, drained carrots, onions and peppers. Mix and serve.

SHORTCUTS
- *Use crinkle cut carrots or baby carrots.*
- *Chop the onion and green pepper together in the food processor.*

HOW SWEET IT IS

1 lb.	cooked carrots, sliced (frozen, thawed carrots are a fine substitute for fresh)
$1/2$ cup	raisins
$1/2$ cup	orange juice
$1/2$ Tbs.	honey (or corn syrup)
1 tsp.	vinegar
1 tsp.	corn starch
$1/2$ tsp.	nutmeg

In a small bowl, mix orange juice with corn starch. Stir well. Add vinegar, honey and nutmeg. Cover and microwave on high for 2 minutes. Stir well. Let cool and pour over carrots.

ZIPPY ZUCCHINI

1 lb.	fresh zucchini, sliced
$10^1/2$ oz.	pkg. frozen corn
4 oz.	can diced green chiles
8 oz.	sharp Cheddar cheese, shredded
1 Tbs.	garlic powder
1 tsp.	salt

Add the above ingredients to a medium, microwaveable bowl. Mix well. Cook in microwave on high for 4 minutes. Zucchini should be firm.

A FRESH LOOK . . .

Vegetables are available year round but differ in price accordingly. Always wash your vegetables well. Cool running water is usually sufficient for above-ground produce. A few of our stand-bys:

- *Asparagus — Look for thin, all-green spears. If the bottom is bulky, white or hard, you're paying for waste. A sauce of mayo and sweet hot mustard is wonderful on this microwaved vegetable.*

- *Peppers — Green, red, yellow or orange, they are good cooked or raw in many dishes, but watch how the prices change with the colors. Summer brings good bargains on green bells. Find a sliced frozen pepper product in the freezer section. Fresh or frozen, they add a quick splash of color to a dish, and are worth the money .*

- *Tomatoes — Buy them firm, unbruised and as red as you can. If you pur-chase them on the green side, place them in a brown paper bag and let ripen on your counter. For the best-tasting tomatoes, GROW YOUR OWN!*

- *Zucchini — It should shine and not be dull. Make sure it's smooth and firm, not soft — with no pitting on the skin.*

- *Mushrooms — For long storage, mushrooms shouldn't be open underneath (exposing the gills). You want a nice tight, sealed cap for that. But for more intense flavor, open mushrooms are more mature. Store in a paper bag — not plastic. Packages of presliced mushrooms save you time but will cost extra.*

FROZEN ASSETS

What's in the supermarket that can make your life more comfortable and simpler? FROZEN FOODS! The freezer section can be the everyday cook's best friend. (It's also Lisa's favorite place during a hot flash.)

Your own home freezer is a resourceful kitchen aid, keeping your frozen vegetables, meats, desserts, plus leftovers and extras for those "ready when you are" meals — sometimes months later!

If you have extra room, freeze water in clean recycled plastic bottles and store in your freezer. It'll help make your freezer more efficient, keep ice convenient for coolers — and provide drinking water in emergencies.

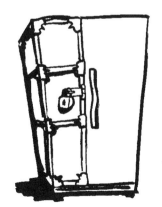

This Ice Queen holds frozen manna — your on-the-run inventory. The Freezer Geezer says, "Fill 'er up. The fuller she is, the better she'll run."

63

HEAVENLY QUICHE

This pie seems to have fallen from the sky, as this "heaven-scent feast" can be freezer-ready to just heat and serve — one for now, one for later.

2	deep frozen pie shells
6	eggs (or egg substitute)
2 cups	low-fat milk
1 cup	lite biscuit mix
1 lb.	Monterey Jack cheese, shredded
1 lb.	sliced mushrooms (fresh, packaged works great)

Remove paper between frozen pie shells (recipe will fill both shells). In medium bowl, add eggs, biscuit mix and milk. Mix well. (If too thick, thin with a little water — if too thin, add more mix.) Add one-half package of cheese and mushrooms to each pie. Salt lightly. Cover each with one-half of liquid. Bake at 325° for about 1 hour.

This recipe is quick to put together. Make two or more and freeze the extra ones. When ready for a quick meal, cover with foil and bake frozen quiche at 400° for 30 minutes or until heated through.

Always make more than you need and keep feeding your freezer.

You feed it and it will feed you!

64

RUSHED CORN BAKE

A great side dish or vegetarian entree.

16 oz.	pkg. frozen corn, thaw and drain
4 oz.	lite cream cheese
4 oz.	jar sliced mushrooms, drained
$1/2$ cup	Swiss cheese, shredded
$1/4$ cup	Italian bread crumbs

A medium casserole dish works well to combine and toss all the above. First, soften the cream cheese for 20 seconds in microwave. Microwave 3 minutes on high, or bake for 15 minutes at 425°. Add some leftover lean meat to vary this dinner.

PASTA STIR-FRY

Here's a delicious, one-dish family meal fit for guests, using frozen, precut vegetables from your supermarket's freezer.

16 oz.	pkg. frozen low-fat vegetables with pasta, thaw first and drain excess liquid
$^1/_2$ lb.	lean beef (or fajita mix) from store's meat counter
1	medium white onion, chopped (or $^1/_2$ cup frozen onion)
3 Tbs.	black bean sauce
2 Tbs.	garlic powder (or jarred garlic)
1 tsp.	powdered ginger
$^1/_2$ cup	sliced almonds (optional)
1 Tbs.	olive oil or nonstick cooking spray

Coat skillet with oil. Over medium heat, sauté onions until translucent. Add meat and garlic. Cook for another 2 minutes. Add vegetable pasta mix. (We recommend thawing first. Adding anything frozen to hot oil can be dangerous.) Stir until all is heated through. Add ginger and bean sauce. Top with sliced almonds.

Blind Sided

At 5:30 P.M., the phone rang in the home office of "The ShortCut Cook." It's our director, Charly. "Uhh, bad news: I just got a phone call. Guess who's NOT coming to dinner?"

See Jane run — the microwave!

Our prized Bay Area celebrity left us high and dry — again! But this time we were ready with a back-up person — just in case.

Jane Trittipo, a microwave cooking author/instructor, was at our doorstep in only thirty minutes — fully and splendidly prepared! She had been put on notice of the possibility of a last minute call. See Jane run! How we love those dependable types! Our "plan B" guest was an "A Number 1 choice."

BRAG ABOUT FRAPPÉ

This is a great make-ahead-and-freeze sweetie! Place a paper doily on the plate beneath the dessert glass and put an Italian cookie alongside to show off this confection.

14 ^{1}/$_2$ oz.	sliced peaches, drain
8 oz.	low-fat ice cream, vanilla or pecan
4 oz.	orange marmalade
1 Tbs.	honey
^{1}/$_2$ tsp.	cinnamon (optional)

Freeze peaches in resealable plastic bag. (Must be frozen to use. Or buy frozen, bagged peach slices.) Add all ingredients to blender. Process until well blended. Pour into two tall glasses. Serve immediately or freeze for later.

CRUMB'Y PEACH COBBLER

There's always room for dessert. This low-cal delight will satisfy even the fussiest palate. Graham crackers aren't just for kids.

2 cups	frozen, sliced peaches (canned peaches work too)
1 cup	(9) low-fat graham cracker crumbs
8 oz.	nonfat peach yogurt
4 Tbs.	sugar (divided use)
1 Tbs.	cinnamon (divided use)

Spray a small microwave dish with nonstick coating. Crumble seven graham crackers to cover the bottom. In medium bowl, mix peaches, cinnamon and 3 tablespoons sugar (make sure they're sweet enough). Layer half the peaches, then half the yogurt. Repeat. Sprinkle two crumbled crackers on top with one tablespoon of sugar and $\frac{1}{2}$ teaspoon cinnamon. Microwave on high for 4 minutes. Let cool and serve in an elegant parfait or martini glass — beautiful, delicious and low-fat!

FREEZER FACTS

Warm up to her frigid ways and turn out meals that "turn on."

- *Freeze foods as quickly as possibly to control bacterial growth.*

- *Store in airtight, moisture- and vapor-proof containers. Label packages with contents and date. Don't try to freeze too many items at one time — that will raise the temperature above the recommended 0° Fahrenheit.*

- *When baking for the freezer — slightly under-cook, reserving any top browning for when you reheat.*

- *With frozen foods, your best buy is one that considers volume, calories, quality **and** price. Don't get caught just reaching for the "lite." READ the label.*

- *Frozen vegetables often are more nutritious than fresh because they are picked and flash-frozen immediately, whereas so-called fresh produce could be sitting around awhile.*

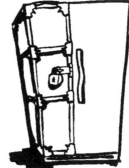

- *Take advantage of sales. Load up your freezer with bargain meats, vegetables, breads, etc., but don't compromise on quality. What goes in must come out — and the deep freeze doesn't do make overs.*

- *Label and organize foods so you won't forget about them.*

REMEMBER

Not all bacterium are killed during freezing. They may become active again during thawing. You should prepare foods as soon as possible after thawing and consume foods as soon as possible after cooking.

FAST CAN BE FRESH

See Jane Run — the Microwave!

When our prescheduled guest pulled the plug on the freezer spot (again), we were left to wonder if there is a "No-Show Guest Spot" — in Siberia? The interview segment's focus changed from the freezer to the microwave (where most frozen foods end up anyway).

Jane Trittipo, our microwave consultant* and author of "The Everyday Gourmet," showed us today that there are fast ways to include fresh produce with your meals — using a microwave.

She says we need to get to know our microwave. The higher the wattage, the faster things cook. It's also an energy saver, efficient and fast in many ways. Even young children should be taught to use this appliance.

* *Jane Trittipo is a chemist and the author of two cookbooks.*

FAST CAN BE FRESH

Jane has 101 tricks in her book— everything from softening hardened brown sugar to drying flowers for potpourri. Here are just a few:

- *Take an ear of corn (leave on the green husk) and microwave for 3 minutes. Let it cool before pulling back the leaves. (The silk comes off very easily now.) Pulling the husk back makes a convenient handle. Arrange on a platter for an elegant summer look.*
- *Cook any combination of fresh vegetable pieces. Arrange the slower cooking ones on the outside of the microwave plate, the faster cooking ones (like zucchini, tomatoes and mushrooms) in the center (in concentric circles).*
- *To accent summer vegetable cooking, first add a flavored oil (like lemon-olive oil) over the top and dust with dry mustard. Add fresh herbs, if you wish, and it will be pretty enough to serve right out of the microwave.*
- *If you are not the gardener type, find the nearest farmers' market for truly fresh produce.*
- *Vegetables are wonderful in the microwave. Don't just use your microwave for warming your coffee. Learn to **cook** with it. This method of cooking vegetables is the healthiest way — preserving the nutrients.*
- *You must be careful to pierce foods that have skins. The waves are attracted to three things: water, sugar and fat. Heating unpierced food can create an explosion.*
- *The best way to peel a tomato is in a microwave. Core the stem. Place on high for 30 to 45 seconds. Let cool and peel. You can do this for peaches too (be sure to pit first).*

With your microwave, you have a dedicated servant waiting on your counter ready for orders, a perfect asset to the harried life.

YUMM-ATOES

Red, juicy and luscious! This beautiful fruit is one of Terrie's favorites, and with the summer season bursting with bountiful harvest — you'd think we could find a decent tomato. Why, it's like trying to find one of those fancy exotic ingredients in a gourmet recipe!

The best-taster comes from someone's vine ripened, home-grown variety — and that probably will always be the case.

Tomatoes from the supermarket are quite often from Mexico, picked green, then "gassed" to turn them red. They are too firm, too tasteless and too expensive! Their beauty runs only skin deep.

*For the best flavor, **grow** your own; "beg, steal or borrow" from a neighbor; or visit your local farmers' market.*

A pale, tasteless tomato is like a bad cup of coffee. Who needs it?

73

ROTUND TOMATOES

4	medium tomatoes (cored), salt inside
¹/₂ cup	frozen petite peas and pearl onions, thawed and drained
¹/₂ cup	bay shrimp, cleaned

Combine dressing below and shrimp mixture, then fill tomatoes. Serve on a bed of lettuce.

2001 ISLAND DRESSING

¹/₂ cup	low-fat mayonnaise
¹/₄ cup	chili sauce
2 tsp.	red pickle relish
¹/₂ tsp.	hot red pepper sauce

In separate bowl, mix all the above.

On Our Side

Lisa's husband Rich also joins the crew today and finally gets to shoot Lisa (with a camera). He replaces another cameraman and adds some needed muscle for set up. Husbands, Rich and Scott (and close friend Brad), lift and navigate our new, but heavy, modular kitchen up two flights of switchback stairs — with much sweat and manipulation.

Then they decorate it, 'mike' it and light it! (We must be dreaming?)

SHORTCUTS

- Select a large, summer-type like beefsteak for these tomato dishes.
- The "2001 Island Dressing" complements shrimp and tomato flavors but you can pair it with **any** summer salad.
- Use center portions of hollowed-out tomato in other recipes (see "Egg-Matoes").
- To encourage tomatoes to drain, salt the inside and set cut-side down. Dressing clings better if tomatoes aren't runny.
- Keep shrimp freezer-ready for the wonderful "Rotund Tomatoes" recipe. They hold one month if properly frozen.
- "Crab is fab" when marinated in the versatile "Lisa's Italian Dressing." Use precooked and cleaned deli crab.
- "Lisa's Italian Dressing" can be used as a dip or drizzle for sliced French bread.

PARSLEY'ED SLICED TOMATOES

The seasoning for this recipe is a knock-your-socks-off, eat-it-up favorite. The flavors are so good, they can make the most of just a little; **even** *with underripe tomatoes.*

4   medium tomatoes sliced ¹/₄" thick

Salt then drain. Arrange on serving plate.

LISA'S ITALIAN DRESSING

1 cup	fresh parsley, no stems
5	garlic cloves
1¹/₂ tsp.	sugar
¹/₄ cup	olive oil
2 Tbs.	red wine vinegar

In miniprocessor, mix parsley and garlic well. Place in small container — top with salt, olive oil, vinegar and sugar. **SHAKE WELL**. Lift parsley mixture with a fork (to get just solids). Spread over tomato slices. Refrigerate. Or, for even tastier tomatoes, serve at room temperature. FABULOUS!

When the taping is over, they strike the set, take out the trash and vacuum! What a labor of love. Now if we can just train them at home . . .

Well, ain't that Rich?

EGG-MATOES

Unscramble the mealtime puzzle. Eggs (or their substitute) are pantry-ready and are a quick fix for a light summertime meal.

2	eggs
$1/2$ cup	diced salted tomatoes (can use centers of "Rotund Tomatoes")
1 Tbs.	garlic powder
2 Tbs.	cilantro
2 Tbs.	chopped onions (can use frozen)
$1/2$ tsp.	lite margarine

In medium, nonstick skillet, heat and add margarine. Scramble all the above in a separate bowl. Add to skillet and cook until egg sets up. Garnish with one tablespoon of cilantro. Also great with our "Sassy Salsa" recipe.

SHORTCUT
*   *No more borrowing eggs from a neighbor — when you stock an egg substitute in your freezer. Ready when you are. Just thaw.*

SALAD DRESS UPS

- A good dressing starts with the best oil — OLIVE OIL. There is a big difference between regular and extra-virgin olive oils. It's the taste! Extra-virgin has a distinct flavor and could dominate a dish. If the label says "lite," it doesn't mean it's light in calories. All oils are 100% fat, so use sparingly. There is also a wide selection of infused-flavor oils that give recipes an easy gourmet touch.

- Vinegars are a must for every cupboard, from the basic red wine to the hearty, tangy or exotic. Experiment with varieties and find which work for you.

- A kitchen staple for making dressing for summer salads is low-fat mayo. (Check labels; lite may not be lower in calories — just fats!) It makes a good Thousand Island dressing with the addition of ketchup, garlic powder and a dash of hot pepper sauce.

- Check out some of the gourmet dressings — definitely an improvement, with trendy flavors like orange basil, champagne and red wine vinegar with thyme. They are fabulous — but they can be high in price and calories! Read the ingredients to see if they contain flavors that you like: cilantro, spices, etc., **then** take the plunge! (You'll want to be pleased after spending a lot of money.)

- Italian (dry packaged mix) dressing should be an essential in your kitchen. It's Lisa's favorite food dress up. Besides making the traditional salad dressing, you can marinate with it using **no** oil. It's also good as an add-in, dry spice mixture. Sprinkle it straight from the package like you would a spice.
- For marinades and dressing, follow package directions, then zip it up even further by adding sweet hot mustard and some honey or sugar. It brings up the flavor a lot without adding fat. Remember fat tastes good to us so you have to keep that **on** your mind (in order to keep it **off** your hips and tummy).
- A salad favorite — bacon pieces, available now with less fat.

- Don't forget to check Appendix B for more great dressing and sauce recipes. Go ahead and take a peek right now!

WHOEVER SAID, "DON'T MAKE WAVES"?

Jane, our microwaving chemist of a guest,* gave us more tips on making use of this time-saving appliance.

Almost 90% of homes have a microwave but people are under-using them. Teach yourself to use it. Depending on your wattage, it's better to "cook and look" and cook again than to make shoe leather. You can always cook some more; just don't overcook it in the first place.

Here are additional hints of what a microwave could do for the everyday cook:

Almond blanching: Place $3/4$ cup almonds and 1 cup water in a micro-safe bowl. Cook on high for 3 minutes. Drain. When cool, rub almonds to remove skins.

Finger nail polish: Loosen a stuck nonmetal cap by microcooking on high for 5 to 10 seconds. With all the time you're saving using shortcut recipes, why not do your nails?

Soften brown sugar: Place box in microwave and cook on high for 30 to 45 seconds.

Peel tomatoes: Core tomato and place in microwave. Cook on high for 10 to 20 seconds. Let stand for a few minutes to cool. Now, peel with ease.

Freshen potato chips: Place stale chips in a micro-safe bowl. Cook on high for 30 to 45 seconds. Let stand for 1 to 2 minutes to crisp.

* Jane Trittipo, author of "The Everyday Gourmet" and "The Marvelous Microwave," is a chemist and microwave cooking instructor.

PIZZA WITH LISA

*This is one of Lisa's favorite fast foods (one of many). There are no rules for success — except, "if you don't like it, don't use it" and "keep your pantry lined with ingredients **you** like."*

Experiment. Throw in a-lot-of-this-and-some-of-that. Get crazy, get cookin' then get out of the kitchen — with these quick-exit recipes.

OPEN THE CUPBOARD DOORS: CREATE A MASTERPIECE

Our dough of choice is a tasty frozen dough. It is versatile, inexpensive and always freezer-ready.

Start with a FOUNDATION.

Frozen bread dough
French bread — all shapes and sizes
English muffins
Tortillas — flour, corn, whole-wheat, your choice
Refrigerated bread or biscuit dough
Sandwich bread slices

Next spread on the SAUCE.

Ready-made sauces, such as pizza and marinara can be full of oil. Make your own fat-free base and save, once again, on calories and money.

For a **tomato** base try:
* *Italian tomato soup*
* *Tomato sauce (canned), sprinkled with dry Italian seasonings.*
* *Tomato salsa, fresh (or dried) cilantro, garlic.*

Short Sided

You'd think we'd be making money by now. HA! The closest we come to money is Lisa "rolling" in the (thawed bread) DOUGH!

We have video tapes to duplicate, supplies to buy — and a dream to fulfill. OK, we did get a kitchen built and a generous local supermarket to provide our ingredients. But we still have tapes to duplicate — and a dream to fulfill.

For a **creamy** base start with:
- *Lite mayo (or that whipped spread that works miracles with sandwiches and salads).*
- *Creamy Italian or ranch-flavored dressing.*

Now build LAYERS.
What's in the fridge? Layer, dump, pile or sprinkle it!

Meats: salami, turkey, pastrami, ham, chicken, leftover whatchamacallit.

Veggies/extras: onions, celery, mushrooms, ripe olives, pineapple, tomatoes — beans?

Add SEASONINGS.
Dry spices: Dry mix Italian dressing, dry Italian herbs, garlic pepper.

Fresh accents: cilantro, rosemary, thyme, basil, ginger?

Finally, TOP it.
Mozzarella — gives it the str-i-i-i-ngy effect.
Cheddar — sharp, tart (need less of this);
*   mild, mellow (may need a little more).*
Monterey Jack — plain or hot-peppered.

BAKE your masterpiece in a preheated oven at 450° until hot (or until the cheese melts).

We are personally financing our hobby and no one feels sorry for us. That's because this is business. And — there's no business like show business!

There are no shortcuts to making money (legally); so we keep our day jobs, to feed this hungry, growing "baby."

And this baby wants PIZZA tonight!

"TO THAI FOR" PIZZA

This highly seasoned round bread makes it really easy to have a homemade pizza in less than thirty minutes. Good way to save money and eat healthily.

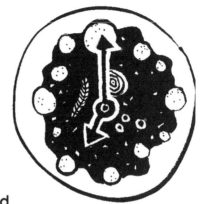

16 oz.	loaf of frozen bread dough, thawed
2	fresh large tomatoes, thinly sliced
2	6 $\frac{1}{2}$-oz. jars marinated artichokes (drain and rinse for fewer calories)
1 cup	low-fat mozzarella cheese, shredded
1 cup	Cheddar cheese, shredded
1 cup	marinara sauce (jar/can, oil free)
1	pkg. dry Italian dressing mix
4 oz.	can sliced ripe olives, drained
8 oz.	low-fat Thai sausage (precooked) nonstick cooking spray

Use a nonstick cookie sheet. Place frozen bread dough in microwave on defrost for 4 minutes. Flatten and roll out bread dough to fit a small cookie sheet. Spread on sauce. Sprinkle on packaged seasonings and cheese. Top with tomato slices and other ingredients. Bake at 400° for approximately 20 minutes. Watch closely — to avoid its burning.

SHORTCUTS

- *While you stretch and pound the dough, TAKE OUT ALL YOUR FRUSTRATIONS!*

- *Don't use "tube type" refrigerator-rolls. They don't turn out the same and have more fat. Save money **and** calories. Use bread dough.*

- *Read the fat content of jar sauce. It takes 8 to 12 oz. to cover one pizza. Buy no oil types.*

- *Using a precooked sausage in this recipe reduces the prep, cook and cleanup. (You don't have to sanitize a cutting board like you would with raw meat.)*

- *Artichoke hearts make this delicious but are packed in oil. Drain and rinse to reduce the fat (or buy canned, water packed).*

- *When selecting a cheese for your pizza, try a reduced-fat version. Be sure to buy dairy items before the "SELL DATE" on the package.*

FLASH RECIPE

TOO-EASY PIZZA SAUCE

Spread on canned tomato sauce then lightly sprinkle on dry Italian seasonings (herbs).

PIZZA IN A PINCH

"Too-Easy Pizza Sauce" and pita bread make this recipe a quick grab-and-go pizza. Great for snacks or meals on the run.

2	pita breads
8 oz.	can tomato sauce
8 oz.	fresh mushrooms, sliced (or canned)
14 oz.	stewed tomatoes (cut in can, drain well)
1 cup	Monterey Jack cheese, shredded
2 Tbs.	Italian seasonings
2 tsp.	garlic powder

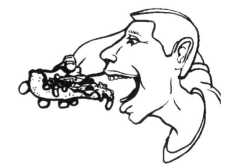

Place whole pita on foil. Layer the above ingredients onto each bread. Start with sauce, season; then add cheese, mushrooms and tomatoes. Bake 5 minutes at 450° on foil.

SHORTCUTS
- *You can freeze large and small pita breads to keep them pantry-ready. The rest of the ingredients are right from your cupboard.*
- *Baking the pitas (as you're warming the oven) before topping them, gives a more pizza-like, crisp crust.*
- *Your own special additions of whatchamacallits will enhance each recipe.*

TOP PIZZA DOG TO THE RESCUE

We wanted to know how to "throw dough around." After eight months on the air, we had become accustomed to stretching it, but throwing it seemed like more fun. Explaining and demonstrating professional pizza maneuvers (with our very low studio ceiling) was Jeff, the master of toss — the quarterback of pizza pitches — the top pizza dog at our favorite parlor.*

- Flour your dough before you begin to flatten it. Press down with your finger tips. Try to keep it round.

- Lift the dough (vertically) and gently stretch out the edges (letting the weight of the piece pull it out even farther). Work your way around the whole circle. While you're doing this, use your whole thumb (down to the palm) to cup extra dough into a ridge at the edge. This forms a nice roll to the edge of your crust and will keep your sauce on the top.

- Lay the dough down again and with your palm flat, press and push outward from the center, moving the dough about a quarter turn each time. Don't get the middle too thin.

- Pick it up: Now you're ready for the big toss in the air. You can do it! Twirl with one hand and catch with the other. This stretches the dough into an even bigger circle.

* Jeff Nixon is a Walnut Creek, California, restaurateur.

- *If you poke or tear it, just lay it on the floured surface and mend it as you would pie crust or any pastry: pinch together, or moisten and overlap with a pinch.*

- *Professional pizza makers sometimes bake the dough on a pizza screen, not a solid sheet. That allows the crust to get crispier. You can purchase one at your local cookware store.*

- *Ladle the sauce in the center and spread it to the edge. Push the sauce along with the bottom of the ladle.*

- *Build up your ingredients so that colors are on top. Put mushrooms on first. Green peppers add a lot of color. Put on tomatoes last.*

- *In a professional pizza oven, it takes only 8 to 10 minutes to bake a pizza pie because of the extremely high heat.*

When ordering your pizza:

- *Ask for half the cheese to save fat calories.*
- *Order a little extra. Cold pizza for breakfast is great!*

TONS OF BUNS

Bread — a basic necessity for the everyday cook. Top it or coat it. Bake it or broil it. It is a staple for the table and a complement to any meal.

49'ER TIGHTENDS

For a football season kickoff, try this quick (10-minute) 97% fat-free chili served on top of a hamburger bun.

1 lb.	97% fat-free turkey meat
8 oz.	stewed tomatoes (half a can), cut up right in the can
15 oz.	can kidney beans, drained
4 oz.	can sliced ripe olives, drained
$1/2$ cup	salsa, see "Sassy Salsa" in index
$1/2$ cup	red onion, chopped
$1/2$ cup	Cheddar cheese, shredded
2 Tbs.	zesty chili powder
2	hamburger buns, sliced

Spray a large skillet with nonstick cooking spray. Brown turkey meat until no longer pink (about 3 minutes). Mix ingredients together (except buns). Simmer an additional 5 minutes. Separate buns. Remove a little of each center and fill with the cooked mixture. Top with onions and cheese. Super with a salad.

From All Sides

Lisa's supermarket bloopers open this show. The food review segment, previously taped in the grocery store, was more funny than informative. So we edited a few cuts to a little slapstick music and set the pace for a really energetic program.

Our first studio guest on this show was a bagel expert — specializing in bagel mayhem! We witnessed five wild minutes of slicing and chopping, spreading and topping.

ITALIAN BREADSTICKS

*Old bread **can** become something new. This is a favorite stand-by recipe. Lisa got the basic idea from a neighbor and adapted it.*

3	**hot dog buns (day-old, best)**
$1/2$ **cup**	**lite margarine, melted**
$1/2$ **cup**	**Parmesan cheese**
	aluminum foil

Place margarine on a paper plate. Microwave for 25 seconds or until melted (careful here). Put cheese on another paper plate. Quarter buns, lengthwise. Brush margarine on each cut side then roll in cheese. Place on foil and bake 4 to 6 minutes at 350° or until lightly browned.

YOU DECIDE:

• *Brushing on margarine = less calories, more time.*

• *Rolling in margarine = less time, more calories.*

He plowed through a mountain of bagels and made about 15 sandwiches. Lisa ate about 12 of 'em. It was mesmerizing to watch. He'd whip one up in 20 seconds. She'd eat it in two.

THINGS YOU KNEAD TO KNOW

We recruited a dietitian* to help us understand the labels on bread. A dietitian and a nutritionist are not the same. Anyone can be a nutritionist (if you eat, you are a nutritionist, of sorts). A dietitian studies premed-type classes for four years, must pass an exam and stay updated every five years.

Read the ingredients on the bread label. If whole-wheat flour is first, the loaf is higher in fiber and has more B vitamins and iron than other breads.

Look at the listing for fiber. Bread **should be** a good source. Three to four grams of fiber is best. You need 25 to 30 grams a day to create a healthy diet. In a whole-wheat bread, you can sometimes see the grains. Don't be fooled by color. It may contain molasses or brown sugar.

Next, look at the fat grams. You want under two grams of fat per serving. Breads need a little bit of fat to make the texture right: Fat makes fewer air holes and causes bread to rise slower. Without fat, bread is really very dry. Most, except for French bread and flat breads, have some fat. French and sourdough are very low in fat, usually .5 grams. But you're not getting much fiber (only 1 gram) for all the calories.

With something like a raisin (English) muffin, you have low-fat (1 gram); some fiber (2 grams); and probably a little bit more iron (from the raisins). So you would get a little better nutrition (for the calorie intake) from a bread like that.

Freezing is the best way to store bread, but wrap it tightly. To thaw, keep it at room temperature. Or heat it in the oven. Microwaving it makes it rubbery and hard to chew. Refrigeration actually dries out bread.

* *Ann Mesaros, R.D., C.D.E., Dietitian at Mt. Diablo Medical Center, Concord, California.*

THIS SPUD'S FOR YOU

Potatoes are nutritious, inexpensive and available year round. They have potassium, Vitamin C and important fiber. Their carbohydrates provide lots of energy. Potatoes can even be a good, healthy snack.

This tuber is worth talking about. It should be a staple in every household since it's always ready for cooking, baking or stuffing. Whether you choose to microwave (REMEMBER TO PIERCE IT FIRST), oven bake, fry, broil or boil, the versatility of potatoes makes this king-carbo one of our favorite foods. Hot or cold, this spud's for you!

This Spud's For You

SHORTCUTS

Baking:

- Microwave four medium potatoes for 10 to 15 minutes on high. Remove and wrap in foil and let stand 5 to 10 minutes.
- For crisper potato skins, microwave as directed above, then slip them into a conventional oven at 350° for 10 minutes.

Boiling:

- The smaller you cut a potato before you boil it, the more nutrients you lose. Cut in half is enough for a small potato. (But if you're in a hurry — 4th's or 6th's. It will cook quicker.)
- Bring water to a boil first, then add your potatoes. That way the water is in contact with the potato less time — so less goodness is lost.
- One pound of potatoes will take about 20 minutes to cook until tender.

Micro-Steaming:

Here's a quick way to prepare spuds for mashing or a speedy casserole.

- Wash and cut up four potatoes (peeling them is optional).
- Place in micro-safe casserole with $1/4$ cup water.
- Cover, cook 15 minutes on high, until tender.

Side Note

*It's a toe-tapping ditty, the knee-slapping medley, of our **very own** "ShortCut Cook" theme song — premiering tonight!*

Simon Russell, talented musician and singer, wrote and performed this in just two days! (You know how we're always in a hurry.) Just in time for our next production day! Great music to cook (and dance) to. Thanks, Simon.

"I say — 'The ShortCut Cook' is here to stay,
'The ShortCut Cook' is gonna show you the way,
'The ShortCut Cook' is what it's all about.
'The ShortCut Cook' is gonna turn it out!

Oh yeah — 'The ShortCut Cook' . . . Sizzle baby,

Ah, we're feeling very 'haute' tonight."

LISA'S SPECIAL

This familiar dish became a favorite, low-fat food-feast. We've taken out most of the fat and upgraded the nutritional value to produce a winner — a complete meal in under 15 minutes.

4	microwaved potatoes (Idaho russet)
1 lb.	ground turkey
10 oz.	box frozen spinach, thawed and squeezed dry (then salt lightly)
4 oz.	mushrooms, can or jar
1 Tbs.	garlic powder
$1/2$ cup	Parmesan cheese
8 oz.	container lite sour cream
10 oz.	can clear vegetable broth
3 Tbs.	low-fat bacon pieces
	nonstick cooking spray

Spray a skillet with nonstick coating. Add turkey. Sauté until almost cooked. Add spinach and all the above ingredients. While mixture is simmering on low, wash four medium potatoes and pierce with a fork. Microwave on high for 12 to 15 minutes. Cool slightly and cut in half lengthwise. Scrape some potato out and mix with the turkey. Scoop meat mixture over potato halves. This really does make a meal!

SHORTCUTS

- *Use turkey breast meat. Watch supermarket ground turkey: It might contain dark meat (and by law, even skin). Buy white meat: It is very low in fat — about 1%, by weight.*
- *Purchase low-sodium products and don't add extra salt if you need to restrict your sodium intake.*

Viewers, as well as Lisa, enjoyed Baby Kendra's guest appearances.

TERRIE'S SPECIAL, TOO

This recipe pairs potatoes with black beans — it's hardy and nutritious, filled with fiber and protein. It takes about 3 minutes to mix and is great for an end-of-the-day fixin'. Everything is pantry-ready!

4	microwaved potatoes
15 oz.	can black beans, drained
11 oz.	can Mexican corn
15 oz.	can stewed tomatoes
2 Tbs.	chili powder
2 Tbs.	garlic powder
1 tsp.	sugar
	Cheddar cheese (optional)

Wash potatoes. Pierce with fork. Microwave about 13 to 15 minutes on high. In medium bowl, add the above ingredients. (Chop stewed tomatoes right in their can to make smaller chunks.) Mix well and microwave 3 minutes or until hot. Scoop out some cooked potato. Fill potatoes with bean mixture. Top with chopped red onion and sharp Cheddar cheese. Delicious and very easy.

ONE POTATO, TWO POTATO

So easy, so good!

4	medium baking potatoes
1 cup	lite sour cream
1/2 cup	sharp Cheddar cheese, shredded
1/4 cup	green onions, thinly sliced

Microwave the potatoes. Cut in half lengthwise. Scoop out inside of potato and mix with ingredients above. (Save some green onion for garnish.) Now, fill each potato skin and microwave for 2 minutes on high.

BEEFY BAKER

No complaints here!

4	whole potatoes, baked
1/2 lb.	extra lean ground beef, cooked
4 oz.	jar sliced mushrooms, drained
2 Tbs.	green onion, chopped (optional)
6 oz.	lite sour cream
	salt to taste

Halve the potatoes lengthwise. Mix all ingredients except potatoes. Heap onto halves and heat in microwave for 2 to 3 minutes on high.

Underside

We are featuring FOUR guests in one show today, all for the humble potato.

Baby Kendra (Terrie's granddaughter) opens the show propped in a potato basket, sucking on a russet. A horticulturist tells tales of the tuber's noble history. Mr. Potato Head introduces Lisa's cooking segment (featuring, what else?, potato recipes) and a home economist explains the varieties of potato along with the do's and don'ts of potato upkeep.

Aye-ya-yi-ya-yiiiii! Guess what, folks? A potato is a potato, is just a P-O-T-A-T-O!

It's humble and should remain that way. We unearthed information enough to write the book, "How to Embarrass a Potato."

POTATO PARADISE
Make in minutes — eat in seconds.

4	microwaved potatoes
1 cup	frozen sliced carrots, thawed
1/2 cup	frozen assorted, sliced bell peppers, thawed and drained
8 oz.	pineapple chunks, drained
4 oz.	can sliced water chestnuts, drained
1/4 lb.	lean deli ham, cubed

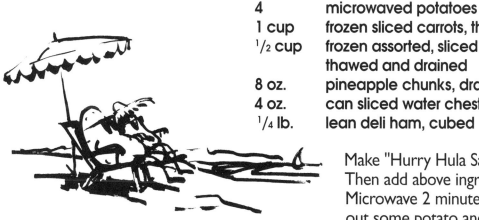

Make "Hurry Hula Sauce" below first. Then add above ingredients. Microwave 2 minutes on high. Scoop out some potato and fill with mixture of sauce, meat, fruit and vegetables.

HURRY HULA SAUCE

1 1/2 tsp.	corn starch
1/2 cup	pineapple juice
2 Tbs.	lite soy sauce
2 Tbs.	honey
1 Tbs.	vinegar

Using pineapple juice, stir in corn starch. Mix well. Add remaining seasonings. Microwave on high for 2 minutes or until thickened.

• *A great sauce with meat balls or stir fry.*

CREAMY POTATO CASSEROLE

This hardy, one-dish meal is a family favorite — it's even better the next day!

4	large potatoes, precooked and sliced
1 lb.	lean ham, or sausage, cubed
1$^1/_2$ cups	frozen petite peas
	"Cream Sauce" (see next page)

Cover the bottom of a 2$^1/_2$ quart microwaveable casserole dish with half of the cream sauce. Layer half the sliced potatoes, half the peas, half the ham or sausage. Top with half the "Cream Sauce." Repeat one more layer in the same order. Cover and microwave on high for approximately 20 minutes. Check halfway through but do not stir.

CREAM SAUCE

3 Tbs.	butter
1	sweet onion, chopped
3 Tbs.	flour
2 cups	nonfat milk
10 $^3/_4$ oz.	can cream of celery soup (98% fat free)
13 $^3/_4$ oz.	can hearts of artichokes (plain, no oil), minced (optional)
$^1/_2$ cup	Cheddar cheese, shredded
1 tsp.	garlic pepper

In a saucepan over medium heat, sauté chopped onion in melted butter until translucent. Add flour and stir. Gradually pour in milk, blending thoroughly. Keep stirring while it thickens. Dump in celery soup, minced artichoke hearts, shredded cheese and garlic pepper. Mix well and let it cook another 5 minutes (keep stirring).

"MEAT ME" AT THE POTATO BAR

The potato can be the start of something big. Truly, this tuber can become the main attraction for lunch or dinner. Just put it on the table and tell your family, "Stuff it!" Here are some pantry-ready suggestions for "tuber topping:"

STUFFERS
Beans, all types**!**
Chili
Deli meats
Deli-cooked chicken
Frozen chicken breasts, thaw, cook, dice
Leftovers
Mushrooms, canned, jarred or fresh
Pineapple chunks
Vegetables, canned, fresh or frozen

DRESSINGS

Blue cheese (see "Blue Cheese Blast" in index)
Broths, thickened with corn starch — quick gravy!
Butter
Salad dressings, prepared
Salsa (see "Sassy Salsa" recipe)
Sauces and Dressings (see Appendix B)
Soups, canned
Sour Cream (lite)

TOPPINGS

Bacon pieces (in a jar, low-fat)
Chives, fresh or dried
Green chiles, canned
Onions: red, white, yellow or green
Ripe olives, sliced (look for jalapeño flavored)
Shredded cheeses, all types work but use lightly
   (or use lite)

'TATER TRIVIA (to be read on the couch)

- Potato cultivation began around 6000 B.C. when Peruvian Indians in the Andes grew them for food — one of the few crops able to be grown at high elevations.

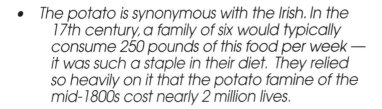

- The next significant period in the history of the potato was when Sir Walter Raleigh brought it to England from the New World. But the plant was misunderstood. Instead of the tuber, the queen's cook prepared the stems and leaves, making everyone very ill.

- The potato is synonymous with the Irish. In the 17th century, a family of six would typically consume 250 pounds of this food per week — it was such a staple in their diet. They relied so heavily on it that the potato famine of the mid-1800s cost nearly 2 million lives.

- The potato chip originated from a Native American cook whose customers complained about thickly cut pieces. The cook cut them "paper thin" before pan frying and the chip was born.

We did Mr. Potato Head proud today. Our guest,* a professional gardener, taught us how to grow the tuber. Now, we can make even a couch potato sprout!

Potatoes are easy to grow but most people don't think of growing them since these tubers are not planted during the primary vegetable planting season. They grow December to February here in California.

So if you get the urge to dig in the dirt and raise your own special, hard-to-find variety of potato:

- *Use seed potatoes. Find them at your local garden center or send away via seed catalogs.*
- *Don't use potatoes from supermarket stock; results can be disappointing. Produce potatoes are treated with a sprout inhibitor to discourage growth and aren't guaranteed to have the genetic characteristics you want.*

Once you decide which variety to grow:

- *Sprout the seed potato by placing in a warm place (away from direct heat) for about 7 to 10 days.*
- *Cut "eyes" into ounce pieces. Leave them exposed to the air 24 to 48 hours to form a callus over the cut portion. Then dip the piece in gardener's dusting sulfur to protect it.*
- *Place eyes in trenches every 8 inches and cover with soil. It's better to plant them in loose, porous soil rather than heavy clay; that causes deformities. The raised bed method (fill an old tire with potting soil or plant directly in a bag of soil) is good.*
- *For tender new potatoes, harvest soon after the plant flowers.*
- *For larger, more mature ones, wait until the foliage has naturally died back (about three months).*

---

* *Buzz Bertolero, "The Dirt Gardener," Navlet's, Inc. nursery and garden centers, Pleasant Hill, California.*

A representative* for the California Certified Farmers' Markets showed us some common-to-rare varieties of potatoes as well as how to take care of them when they follow us home.

Russet — most popular baking potato. It is mealier and so bakes up fluffy.

Yukon Gold — great to boil. Moist inside — to eat as is or to mash. These are flavorful.

Red Boiling Potatoes or Petite Red — just scrub and cook as they are. You don't need to peel them. These are so easy to microwave.

Russian Banana — a long narrow yellow variety. Moist inside. A novelty — they're fun to work with.

Yellow Finns — a round yellow type, high in moisture so they do not store well.

Butterball — another moist yellow type (gobble these up).

Keeping An Eye On Potatoes:

- *When buying, purchase a quantity to last one to two weeks. Don't expect to keep them a month.*
- *You shouldn't refrigerate any raw potato. The starch will convert to sugar, causing browning in the center. Place in an open weave basket — in a dark, cool spot. Fifty degrees is the ideal temperature for storing potatoes.*

* Barbara Kobsar, home economist, columnist, community relations/Farmers' Markets, author.

NO-SWEAT SWEETS

When you keep things on hand, it's easy to make a great dessert in less than 3 minutes. You can make a nice presentation with pantry-ready ingredients.

NO-PUDGE FUDGE CAKE

This is a no-guilt cake, 'cause it takes no time to prepare. The fat goes but the flavor stays.

1	fat-free pound cake, cut ¹/₃ inch slices
4 oz.	jar chocolate fudge
4 oz.	jar marshmallow creme (microwave 30 seconds to soften)
¹/₂	banana, thinly sliced

Sandwich style, spread a slice with a tablespoon of fudge. Cut banana pieces on top. Place another slice on that. Top with a tablespoon of marshmallow creme and drizzle fudge over it.

DIG-IN DESSERT

It looks like you're digging in dirt but it's scrumptious chocolate. This make-and-freeze dessert is impressive to have on hand.

4	4-inch terra cotta (clay) pots, washed
¹/₂ quart	low-fat vanilla ice cream
12	chocolate, vanilla cream sandwich cookies (reduced fat)
4	plastic flowers

Side Splitting

"I don't care HOW much you eat . . . NO FAT HERE!" Lisa says, to the camera, with tears flowing down her face. She's laughing uncontrollably and has lost all composure. Even the cake she is making is losing its gooey ground. Under the hot studio lights, the fudge and marshmallow creme have turned into a lava flow and the cake into a land slide!

"No-Pudge Fudge Cake" is the messiest, stickiest dessert ever to be allowed on the airwaves.

*Lisa's fingers are coated in marshmallow creme and she succumbs to the inevitable, edible temptation. Her fingers go into her mouth and onto her face leaving a sticky residue of white goo. She gets us **all** laughing now, as she relates her childhood reputation of always being called "Dirty-face Lisa."*

We learned a valuable lesson tonight. A good laugh is good for the soul and — good for the show. We'll just keep those cameras rolling!

Place one cookie in the bottom of each pot to cover hole. Add ice cream to one inch from the top. In a miniprocessor, grind 8 cookies until they resemble dirt. Sprinkle the cookie crumbs on top of each pot of ice cream. Cover with foil. This can be frozen for a few days. When you're ready to serve, let stand at room temperature for about 15 minutes. Insert one flower into each pot. For an extra treat, hide a "gummy worm" candy in the ice cream!

QUICK 'N' CRUNCHY GRANOLA TOPPING

Try this over fresh or canned fruit or ice cream; add it to cookie dough for crunch; or eat it by itself with a little milk.

2 Tbs.	butter
1/2 cup	brown sugar
1 cup	quick cooking oatmeal
2 oz.	pkg. sliced almonds
2 Tbs.	sesame seeds (optional)

In a nonstick skillet, melt butter and brown sugar. Add oatmeal, almonds and sesame seeds. Cook over medium-high heat for about 2 minutes, stirring constantly. Remove from heat and cool.

HARRIED BERRY DESSERT

This is our version of a popular sweet stand-by dessert. It's so easy even children can make it. Canned fruit will work too.

16 oz.	pkg. unsweetened frozen peaches
16 oz.	pkg. unsweetened frozen black berries
1	small pkg. any flavor gelatin
9 oz.	white cake mix (half of a 1 pound, 2 ounce box)
$^1/_2$ cup	oatmeal, uncooked
6 Tbs.	butter, sliced
$^1/_2$ cup	sliced almonds (or walnuts)

Place frozen fruit in a 11" x 7" microwaveable dish. Sprinkle flavored gelatin over fruit. Cover fruit with dry cake mix, oatmeal and almonds. Top with sliced butter. Lightly cover with plastic wrap and microwave on high for 15 minutes (10 minutes for canned fruit). Meanwhile, preheat oven to 350°. Remove from microwave and take off plastic wrap. Cover with foil and **bake in oven** for another 15 minutes (10 minutes for canned fruit). Remove foil and let brown an additional 5 minutes. Serve by itself or as a topping over ice cream.

Greg Thurston,* a professional body builder and personal fitness trainer, joined our "No-Sweat Sweets" interview segment.

We asked him the proverbial question, "How can we have our cake and eat it too?" His response, "EXERCISE!" (Duh.) So how do we find time to exercise when we hardly have time to think? He says, "Just do it."

Greg believes one of the important things in helping people reach fitness is determining their personal goals.
- *Sometimes reaching a goal means some lifestyle CHANGES.*
- *Examine your entire week, a day at a time: lifestyle, activities and any exercise regimen — from the time you get up until you go to bed.*
- *It's important to design a routine that's really going to work for you. It's helpful to write everything down from Monday to Sunday, your activities and everything you eat — even if it's candy.*

HERE'S a surprise
- *Sometimes what people think they're doing wrong isn't really so bad — it might not be hurting them. It could be other things they're not doing.*
- *Find out what's in the foods you do eat. Get a book of food values and make it your reference.*
- *Know how many calories, and how much fat and sodium you are eating. Fat free is good, of course, but excess calories (of any kind) can be bad.*

* Greg is the owner of Mobile Fitness, Danville, California.

- *Be aware of what you put into your body.*
- *You are still going to have cravings. It's better not to ignore them. Allow yourself some food luxuries two days a week, say on the weekend. Be good the rest of the week. So it's O K to look forward to eating anything you want, then getting back on track Monday.*

The OTHER important fact is stay active.
- *Think back to your childhood — what did you get out and do that was play? Did you go to the beach, shopping (walking) at the mall? It's all about getting up and moving.*
- *Walking is one of the best exercises because it doesn't take special equipment or location. Just go someplace you like. Make it an enjoyable outing — take your family and spend time together. Invite some friends for a walk, a swim or to play golf, instead of thinking, "I don't have time to 'get into' a workout program." Combine things. Apply exercise to family and social time.*

THERE is aerobic and anaerobic exercise.
- *Do what you are able to do even if it's not "normal" exercise. If it's raining, consider walking (up and down your stairs) or doing squats (from your chair — sit down then stand up, etc. — while you watch T V).*
- *You can do anaerobic exercises (weight resistance) by using your pantry-ready canned goods or milk jugs instead of dumbbells. You don't need special equipment. This exercise strengthens and tones muscles.*
- *Aerobic exercise, such as walking, conditions the heart and lungs.*
- *It's best to do SOMETHING. Anything is better than nothing.*

THANKSGIVING AT THE BISTRO

This was one of our favorite shows because someone else was doing the cooking. We firmly believe that no one should have to cook ALL THE TIME. Everybody, sooner or later, needs a break. So, we went on location to the Sunrise Bistro in Walnut Creek, California, where we experienced, firsthand how Cindy Stein (owner and chef) DAILY prepares Thanksgiving recipes, year around – the easy way!

It's business as usual at the Bistro when a customer orders a full turkey dinner, with all the trimmings. It is one of Cindy's most popular menu items . We asked her to share her expertise, and recipes, to help make this holiday feast a little easier on everyone, including us.

She suggested that instead of getting a "bad attitude" during the holiday rush, you get everyone to help. Put them to work. To reduce stress, get things ready and out of the way well ahead of time. Prepare foods a day or more in advance. Many recipes (in part or in whole) can be made ahead. The Thanksgiving Day meal is no exception.

Take the heat out of the kitchen and a load off your feet. Get shopping then cooking prior to the actual eat-like-a-pig day. (Or, better yet, get invited to someone else's home.)

OVEN-ROASTED TURKEY BREAST

- *If you're feeding just a few: Consider purchasing only that part of the turkey you'll eat. Whole cavity (breast plus back) cooks a lot faster than an entire bird (about 2 $^1/_2$ hours at 375°). Most customers of the Bistro choose white (breast) over dark meat. That's good since breast meat is low in fat.*

- *If you buy a whole turkey: Cut off the legs and wings and lay them around the breast to use later for broth and soups. Crack the cavity and slightly flatten it.* Cut up raw carrots and onion, and place inside.*

- *If you're cooking ahead: After roasting and cooling the bird, pull half the breast off the bone in one piece. Slice across-the-grain thinly, using a serrated knife. All this can be done the day before. Reheat it in a shallow pan with some broth. This takes about 15 minutes at 300° and steams it — just like freshly roasted. Display on a plate for serving.*

*This stops the cavity from rolling around in the pan.

Set Aside

The work is never done but we need to take occasional breaks! And being "girls (who) just wanna have fun," we decided to throw a Thanksgiving party and tape the festivities. What better time to thank our families and volunteer crew for their continued support and hard work (and take a shortcut by creating a fresh show in the process)?

Cindy's Bistro offered us a haven for the evening. Simon Russell, our composer of "The ShortCut Cook" theme song, graced us with his melodies.

We hardly ever take time-outs! Terrie and Lisa encourage all our viewers and readers to take some special time for just YOU. Yes, kids need quality time but so do you.

We finished that evening's taping with full tummies and lightened hearts as Simon closed the evening singing "Amazing Grace."

And gee, we WERE amazed. A year has almost passed and we're all looking forward to the next.

*Don't give in to the hustle and bustle or **hassle** of the season we're now entering. Hang on. Keep looking up!*

HERBED SAGE STUFFING

Stuffing secrets straight from Cindy's grandmother.

1 lb.	herbed bread, torn into small pieces
3 Tbs.	butter
1 Tbs.	sage
1 Tbs.	celery seed
1	large red onion, diced
1 cup	celery, diced
$1/2$ tsp.	curry powder
$1/2$ cup	chicken broth

In medium skillet, add celery and onion. Sauté lightly in butter. Add seasonings, bread and broth. Stir and simmer another 5 minutes.

SHORTCUTS
- *Use herbed bread that's a few days old.*
- *Encourage your children to help with this task. They like tearing the bread into little pieces.*
- *Save your fat calories for dessert. Instead of sautéing in butter, use chicken broth.*
- *Cindy prefers to cook the stuffing separately. She offers this tip for those who love it cooked in the turkey. Make the stuffing a day in advance and refrigerate it in its mixing bowl. Never stuff the bird with the warm (or even room temperature) stuffing. To avoid bacterial growth.*

GAR-LICKED RED POTATOES

This low-fat recipe lets you save calories for gravy!

2 lbs.	petite red potatoes
5	cloves garlic, peeled
1/4 cup	low-fat milk
	salt to taste
1 Tbs.	butter (for extra flavor)

In medium pot, add a cup of water. Simmer potatoes (cut into small pieces to reduce cooking time) with garlic. Drain water when potatoes are well cooked, keep the garlic. Add milk and mash with fork.

HOMEMADE CRANBERRY SAUCE

Cindy likes to involve family. This is one her children like to do; it's so easy, but it's a recipe that makes everyone think you really worked.

1 lb.	fresh, whole cranberries
1/2 cup	sugar
1/2 cup	orange juice

In medium sauce, add cranberries, sugar and orange juice. Cook on medium-low heat for about 15 minutes. Cook berries well so they will gel.

Side Order

A reflection on Thanksgiving: We have a lot to be thankful for. We have faithful families and good friends.

APPLE PIE

This apple pie is a healthier alternative to the traditional pumpkin pie (with its evaporated milk and eggs). It takes about TWO HOURS to make — but it's worth the wait. The aroma alone "warms the house."

1	**pkg. frozen, deep-dish pie crust (made with vegetable oil) or make your own**
6	**Granny Smith apples (firm)**
1 cup	**sugar**
2 Tbs.	**lemon juice**
1 Tbs.	**cinnamon**
2 Tbs.	**flour**

Coat apples with sugar, lemon juice, cinnamon and flour. Pack tightly in pie crust. This will look overstuffed. While still in its pie tin, turn the second crust over (on top of the filled one) and release the pastry. **Seal** edges by pinching together. Be certain to make large slits in top of pie crust to vent while baking. Bake at 325° for 1 hour, 40 minutes. Remove pie from oven. Let cool one-half hour. Reinsert knife in slits before cutting if serving right away.

IT'S AS EASY AS APPLE PIE

- *Granny Smith apples work best in making an apple pie. They are **firm** and **tart**. Adding the **sweetness** of cinnamon and sugar makes them delicious.*
- *You can prepare apples the **day before**. Just add lemon juice to them. Refrigerate to keep them from turning brown.*
- *To get more juice from the lemon, roll it between the counter top and the heel of your palm. Lean on it as though you were kneading bread. Squeeze out the whole lemon over the sliced apples.*
- *Try leaving on the apple skins. It's healthier, easier and quicker. It helps give **texture** to the pie because the fruit pectin is just under the skin.*
- *Slice the apples thin. It takes about six medium apples for a nine-inch, deep-dish pie shell.*
- *Apples shrink a lot. Don't be afraid to really pile them up!*
- *If you make your own crusts, place them in foil pie plates. **Store them** in the freezer. Another option is to purchase already-made crusts (although many contain vegetable shortening). Cindy* prefers butter in her recipes.*

* Cindy Stein is chef/owner of Sunrise Cafe and Bakery, Walnut Creek, California.

LOVIN' LEFTOVERS

Being invited to someone else's home for the Thanksgiving Day meal has one disadvantage — NO LEFTOVERS!

As shortcut cooks, we need to take advantage of the week-long, post Thanksgiving tradition. It is that wonderful time of the year when American families **welcome** *the idea of eating leftovers. They are happy to pick off the spent carcass and eat turkey sandwiches two or three times a day — ALL WEEK LONG.*

If you did not plan to cook a turkey dinner, it may not be too late. And, yes, it is worth the effort.

TASTY TURKEY BREAST

Tastes great with "Cornbread Stuffing."

2 lb.	fillet of turkey breast, remove skin
$^1/_2$	package onion soup mix (dry)
4 oz.	can sliced mushrooms, drained
$^1/_4$ cup	cream sherry

Preheat oven to 450°. Coat turkey with onion soup mix. Place in a nonstick baking dish. Pierce turkey several times with a fork to tenderize. Pour canned mushrooms over, then add sherry. Cover with foil and cook for 20 minutes. Check for doneness by piercing the center of the meat with a knife. Juices should run clear.

Allow to cool, then slice thinly. Serve with your favorite low-fat gravy and canned whole cranberries. Makes for great sandwich fixin's.

CORNBREAD STUFFING
Lovin' spoon-fulls!

3 cups	cornbread stuffing mix
14 oz.	can chicken broth
1 cup	frozen corn
4 oz.	can diced green chiles, drained
$^3/_4$ cup	chopped walnuts
1 tsp.	chili powder
1 tsp.	sugar

Spray medium casserole dish with nonstick cooking spray and add all above ingredients. Mix well. Preheat oven to 450° for 10 minutes. Bake casserole for 15 minutes. If you want firmer stuffing, add one egg to mixture. Salt and pepper to taste.

SHORTCUT
* *Microwave it! In medium bowl, heat broth to a near boil. Pour in stuffing mix. Blend well. Add remaining ingredients and cook on high for 1 $^1/_2$ minutes.*

Terrie's caught taking a rare break between taping.

APPLE SWEET POTATOES
Apples can really add a tartness to sweet potatoes.

15 oz.	can sweet potatoes (or 2 cups leftover) drained, sliced
3	Granny Smith apples, cored and sliced
3/4 cup	brown sugar
1/4 cup	lite margarine
1/4 cup	white sugar

In medium, nonstick casserole dish, place half the potatoes and apples. In a small microwaveable bowl, mix sugars and margarine. Heat until softened. Drizzle half the mixture over casserole. Repeat apple potato layer. Top with remaining sauce. Microwave for 6 minutes or until apples are cooked. Serve with turkey, roast chicken or pork. Delicious!

YAM IT UP

This quick casserole can be made from fresh or canned yams. Actually, this recipe complements more than turkey. It goes well with ham, pork loin or chicken.

2	13-oz. cans yams, drained (or cooked sweet potatoes)
17 oz.	can lite apricots (save half the juice)
6 oz.	bag dried fruit bits
$1/2$ cup	brown sugar
2 tsp.	cinnamon

Spray microwaveable bowl or small casserole dish with nonstick cooking spray. Cover bottom of the dish with one can of yams. Arrange half of apricots on top. Sprinkle with $1/4$ cup of brown sugar, half the bag of fruit bits and 1 tsp. cinnamon. Repeat the layers. Microwave for about 7 minutes. Mmm!

SHORTCUTS
* *Chop the apricots right in the can.*
* *Substitute fresh or leftover sweet potatoes for the canned yams.*

CRANBERRY DELIGHT

Make your own cranberry side dish: It's easy!

3	15-oz. cans whole cranberries
8 oz.	cornflakes, crushed

Mix the following:

3/4 cup	brown sugar
1/2 cup	lite margarine, melted
1 tsp.	cinnamon

Spray a small cake pan with nonstick coating. Spread one can of cranberries over bottom. Crunch corn flakes over this and drizzle with sugar mixture. Repeat for two more layers. Bake uncovered for 12 to 15 minutes at 375°, just until bubbly. Serve as a sauce to accent your turkey or serve as dessert over vanilla ice cream.

SHORTCUT

- *Use leftover cranberries, **if** you have any!*

LISA'S LEFTOVERS

*Day-late and dollars-ahead dinners are accomplished by combining already-cooked foods with items from your cookin' cupboards. By adding just a few **new** ingredients (like sautéed onions, frozen vegetables, fresh or dry herbs, a quick sauce or can of soup) you can lighten your cooking load and "dish it out" in minutes. Leftovers are an important kitchen asset — on any given day. It's a great way to jump-start a meal.*

PLAN ON LEFTOVERS
While you're at it (cooking that is), make the most of your time by making EXTRAS.

ENCORE REQUESTS
Double or triple whatever you cook. Put it in a storage container, label, date and freeze. Resealable plastic bags work great, even for liquids! They lay flat.

In just a few minutes, you can easily defrost and heat directly in the bag (open it for ventilation) using your microwave. This method gives you a good head start on any casserole creation or side dish.

Lovin' Leftovers

Word of caution: Don't be overzealous. Spending hours making extras is not our idea of saving time or making life easier. If it takes a whole day, you probably won't do it again. Also, if you can't eat frozen leftovers within a month or two, you probably won't eat them at all. Ease into this process, a little at a time, and make it work **for** you.

IN COLD STORAGE
Out of sight, out of mind?
Out of reach, hard to find?

If we could, we would invent a color-reactive storage container and call it "Going-Going-Gone." It would use the same concept as the mood ring. (You remember those!) This special container would automatically change its outside color in relation to the inside contents — and their current stage of mutation. No waste. No surprises. Just lots of swirling colors telling us **when** it's time to eat **what**.

In the meantime — designate a **shelf** in your freezer for leftovers!

Here are professional turkey tips on preparing, cooking and carving a tasty turkey, from Brian* (one of our favorite butchers at Diablo Foods in Lafayette, California).

SHOPPING

- *Consider the (Bay Area's own) fresh, all-natural "Willie Bird." This turkey has no additives or preservatives and is noted for being a large breasted bird and having a lot of white meat.*

- ***Plan** on having leftovers, so buy about 1¹/₂ pounds of turkey for each person.*

PREPARING

- *When preparing fresh turkey, briefly bring the bird to room temperature. Otherwise, if it's straight from the refrigerator, the outside will cook fast while the inside will just be getting warmed up.*

- *Stuff slices of red delicious apples and yellow onions inside the neck and cavity. Rub olive oil over the skin and sprinkle with lemon pepper.*

COOKING

- *A real shortcut in roasting a turkey is using a foil pan with reinforced bottom. Place in pan, breast side UP. Cover loosely with foil. Baste about every 45 minutes with its own juices.*

- *Don't overcook the bird: 12 to 15 minutes per pound at 325° is adequate. Use a meat thermometer (don't rely on a pop-up timer).*

- *Remove foil during the last 45 minutes of cooking time, to brown evenly.*

* Brian King, butcher, Diablo Foods, Lafayette, California.

CARVING

- Move things out of the way. Give yourself plenty of room. Carving is easier if it's a one-person affair. Clear everyone out so you don't get stage fright.

- It's important to use a knife you are comfortable with. Family heirloom silver or fancy carving sets may not be the best choice.

- To separate the thigh from the drumstick, pull slightly. Then run the knife down that separation. Pull as you cut. Just cut the thigh across the grain and serve the drumstick "as is."

- Leave on the wings as support so the turkey won't wobble. Start with the breast. Cut on a downward slant, parallel to the breast bone and toward the wing.

A TISKET, A TASKET: PACK A HOLIDAY GIFT BASKET

The holiday spirit has arrived — and it is rattling its chains. Money's tight. The long lists of "to dos" are haunting us and the long lines in shopping malls are giving us a bad attitude.

This chapter is dedicated to: Time-Savin'-Money-Savin'-Penny-Pinchin'-Make-It-Wrap-It-Just-Give-It GIFTS. Whew! It's easier to make it than say it.

*Instead of becoming a **basket** case this season — give one. These personalized, homey gifts take only minutes to make and are packed with good cheer. Avoid the long lines of shopping. Involve the whole family and help bring back a better spirit to the winter holidays.*

SWEET WHEATS

*In*expensive, *in*novative and *in*to your gift basket.
The trick is keeping them **out** of your mouth!

6 cups	puffed wheat cereal
2 cups	dry roasted peanuts
$^{1}/_{2}$ cup	brown sugar
2 Tbs.	honey
1 Tbs.	butter (optional)
	nonstick cooking spray

Add the puffed wheats and peanuts to a large bowl.
In a medium, microwaveable bowl, combine butter
(optional) sugar and honey. Microwave for 45
seconds on high or until liquid. Stir the heated sugar
mixture well. Pour over wheat puffs and peanuts and
toss (mix with hands if it's not too hot). Spray
cookie sheet with a nonstick spray. Spread out
"Sweet Wheats" mixture on pan and bake for 10 to
12 minutes at 350° degrees. Watch closely. You
don't want to burn something this yummy. Cool.
Store in an airtight container.

South Side

*We've been riding this production
merry-go-round for eleven months
now and no matter how much we kick
and scream, we can't seem to get
anywhere. Friends and family ask us
where we think this is going —
besides in circles. We're frustrated by
our natural creative drive but lack
direction.*

*We're going to break this cycle.
Armed with our video camera, we've
decided to attend the Los Angeles
Cable Convention to capture some
footage for our show and a little
needed fun for ourselves.*

*VIP television executives attend each
year searching for great programs
(like ours). Major cable companies,*

with elaborate displays, show off their latest television series and famous stars. With glitz and glamour they throw dazzling theme parties to strut their magnificent stuff.

The hundreds of dollars it costs to attend can't compare to the thousands the cable industry will spend to pursue a VIP.

So why are we there? The free booth prizes! Tee-shirts, pencils, notepads, bags, buttons and no-brainer games (that anyone can play and win).

Yes, we brazen babes, dressed like VIPs, wait hours in long lines to load up on basket stuffers. We've got our priorities straight!

ROLLIN' IN THE CHEESE BALL

Have a ball making this great basket stuffer. It's as tasty to eat as it is messy to create. Make sure you have clean hands — and short sleeves!

8 oz.	pkg. lite cream cheese
4 oz.	sharp Cheddar cheese, shredded
1 Tbs.	garlic powder
1 Tbs.	Worcestershire sauce
$1/3$ cup	chopped walnuts (and/or fresh parsley)

To soften cream cheese in microwave, unwrap and place in microwaveable bowl. Heat 15 to 30 seconds until soft (don't melt). Add Cheddar cheese, garlic powder and Worcestershire sauce, then the dry ranch-flavored dressing to the cream cheese and mix well. Shape into a ball and roll in walnuts (and/or parsley). Wrap well in plastic. Place dated sticker on gift saying: "Must refrigerate."

SHORTCUTS
* Make this for your own party, add it to a holiday basket, or, if you're lucky enough to be invited to someone's home, bring this with crackers as an appetizer .

131

LIFT-OFF COFFEE

*"5 ... 4 ... 3 ... 2 ... 1 ... Blast off!" Perk up your
basket (or your own morning cup'a) with this fast-
make-up gift that gives a lift.*

1 cup	instant coffee (regular or decaf)
1 cup	nonfat powdered milk
$1/2$ cup	sugar
2 tsp.	ground cinnamon

Combine all the above. Mix well.
Store in an airtight container.
Directions for use (include when
giving as gift): Add one tablespoon
of "Lift Off Coffee" to one cup of
hot water.

SHORTCUTS

- *Measure and mix right in a resealable plastic
bag. (Make sure it is tightly closed.)*
- *To tranquility: As you sip this coffee — try to
forget about traffic jams, mean people and
waiting in long lines to spend money you
don't have. Instead, think about snow and
fun; fireplaces, presents (gift baskets) and
children frolicking — quietly. If you still can't
envision it — this recipe can accommodate
a little brandy!*

GREAT BALLS O' WHISKEY

14 oz.	pkg. large vanilla wafers
3 Tbs.	cocoa powder
3 Tbs.	corn syrup
1¹/₂ cup	pecans, chopped
¹/₄ cup	whiskey
1 cup	powdered sugar

In blender or food processor, add wafers and pecans. Chop finely. Mix in all other ingredients and shape into cherry-sized balls. Roll in powdered sugar. Store in airtight container in the refrigerator. Good cold.

SUBSTITUTION:

Rum can be used instead of whiskey. Or use pure vanilla for a nonalcoholic cookie.

QUICK CARAMEL QUACK'R SNACKERS

Consider doubling this recipe. They seem to get snatched before they're hatched!

¹/₄ cup	light brown sugar
¹/₄ cup	white sugar
¹/₄ cup	corn syrup
2 Tbs.	butter (or lite margarine)
1 tsp.	vanilla
1 bag	microwave popcorn, popped

Mix first five ingredients and microwave on high until the mixture is bubbly and butter is melted. Pour over popped corn. Distribute evenly. Coat a cookie sheet with nonstick spray. Spread out the mixture and bake at 350° for about 10 minutes.

Lisa's nephew, Dan, plates beautiful "finished dishes" but he is also an enthusiastic "Floor Director."

FLASH RECIPE

TEA FOR TWO

¹/₂ cup	instant tea
2 Tbs.	orange-flavored instant drink mix
2 tsp.	allspice

Besides a great basket filler, a single serving (sealed in a decorative mug) is a thoughtful hostess gift.
To serve, mix 1 tablespoon into 1 cup of hot water.

134

OVER-THE-COUNTER CONTAINER IDEAS

When you find yourself in the midst of the rabid shopping crowds, remember one thing: it's each to his own, "survival of the get-its." Our guest* looks for bargain baskets, decorative containers and goodies. They could be right under your nose. Keep in mind the recipients and what treats they might best enjoy.

Wash all containers that will hold food, before adding the goodies. Make sure you wrap foods, tightly and well, with a good-quality plastic wrap. Use lidded, sealing jars to keep foods like "Sweet Wheats" or nuts, fresh.

BASKETS: Differently shaped baskets are available and don't have to be expensive. Try your local thrift store for a bargain. (Make sure they are clean.)

LITTLE BOXES: Fill with goodies and decorate.

JARS: Available in all sizes, colors and prices. Interesting shapes are fun. Collect jars from supermarkets, thrift and discount stores. Look for jars with rubber gaskets to keep your food gift airtight and fresh. Clear containers look best when they are completely filled.

MUGS: Can make a beautiful gift container. Fill one with a dry mix like "Lift Off Coffee" or "Tea For Two." Seal it well with clear plastic wrap before any decorative wrap.

GIFT BAGS: Also available in many sizes and colors. Gift bags are good alternatives to using willow or wicker baskets.

* Hilda Bjerke, owner Bjerke & Assoc., corporate gift baskets, Danville, California.

JAR OR MUG "DRESS UP"

Use Mylar "paper" (same stuff shiny balloons are made of) to dress up a plain container. Buy Mylar in many different colors at most craft stores. Or cut up a used Mylar balloon.

(Open containers need to be wrapped securely, before decorating.)

1. *Cut a square piece, larger than the container lid, to make a decorative "dust cover." Mylar is slippery so hold tightly.*
2. *Use a rubber band over the Mylar to secure it around the rim.*
3. *Cover the band with curling ribbon. Be sure to knot it tightly.*
4. *Curl the ends. This is pretty enough to give without a gift bag. Just tie a tag on it and it's ready to place on your host's table or under the Christmas tree.*

A TISKET, A TASKET:
TRIM YOUR HOLIDAY GIFT BASKET

The previous chapter showed how easy and inexpensive it is to make your own gift basket goodies. Now we suggest some popular basket stuffers that you can buy. Put it ALL together and add the finishing touches for a special, festive look.

DECORATING YOUR GIFT BASKET

FESTIVE FILLERS:

1. Cut a rectangle of Mylar (any size).
2. Fold two diagonal tips together.
3. Pinch at the crease directly below the tips and hold it.
4. Tuck the bottom point of Mylar into your closed fist — just a little ways.
5. Fluff out the tips so they all point UP.
6. Secure the bottom with a floral stick (the ones with wires attached) or use a twist tie.
7. Nestle it among the excelsior (or shredded waxed paper filler) between the gifts.

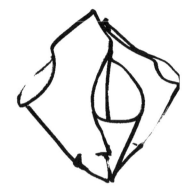

SUGGESTED BASKET FILLERS

Flavored coffee	Stationery
Balloons	Jams and Jellies
Salami	Biscotti cookies
Ham	Salsa
Candies	Lottery tickets
Sauces	Champagne
Napkins	Small games
Cheeses	Nuts
Smoked salmon	Chocolates
Oils	Popcorn
Crackers	Olives
Vinegars	Canned oysters
Sweet Hot Mustard	Wine

- A good way to pack a basket is to fill the bottom with scrunched up tissue paper or unprinted newspaper. (Contact your local newspaper for "end bolts" when the printing day is done.)
- Arrange your decorated gifts securely.
- In a big basket, fill it with several small items.
- Hide the bottom layer "filler," using commercial shredded waxed paper, excelsior or shredded Mylar. This dresses up the top of the basket after you've tucked in your goodies.

FANCY BOW

The most important part of decorating your basket is making the bow according to our guest.* Fancy bows are costly but you can make one easily. It won't take more than two minutes — once you get the hang of it.

Buy ribbon at a craft store.

1. *For a large basket: make a 'roll' of the loose ribbon that measures about five inches in diameter. Make at least 10 layers (this will create 5 bow 'loops' on each side of the center).*

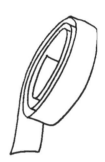

2. *Flatten the roll and crease the two ends.*

3. *Fold the flattened roll in half.*

* Hilda Bjerke, Bjerke & Assoc., corporate gift baskets, Danville, California.

4. Cut the corners at the fold, a third of the width, (leaving the middle third of the folded ribbon edge intact).

5. Carefully open the roll back up to an 'O' shape. Tie the notches together with a pipe cleaner.

6. To fluff the bow, take one side of loops at a time and pull one loop **UP** and the next one **DOWN**. Twist each in an opposite direction to create fullness.

Other decorating ideas:
- Add some craft store fruit or vegetable "pics."
- Collect pine cones and place between gifts.
- Use "silks" — stems of greenery that look like pine boughs, poinsettias or cranberries, etc.

Keep on Cookin'!

Thank you for coming along with us on our shortcut journey to healthy and timely cooking. Little did we know when we first took on the challenge of helping the everyday cook that we would be writing a book — after **three years** of production!

We trust that our recipes, sidelines and tips will give you solutions that will lighten you heart as well as your kitchen work load. We're sure you already know that one of the best things for you, besides food, is laughter. (And our first year on television was **hilarious**.)

As we ended that year, in awe, and began to tackle a second, with vim and vigor (or is that spit and vinegar? Well, we're **sure** it's at least vinegar!), we realized we had learned just enough — to get us into trouble.

Our next book is sure to provide more delicious fun as we share with you our scrumptious recipes, timesaving shortcuts and wacky food adventures — of Year Two.

We hope that we have encouraged you to start "playing with your food!"

Remember: If you have to do something at least three times a day, why not make it **FUN**, *FAST* and **HEALTHY**?

God bless.

Expedient Ingredients
(Convenience, convenience, convenience!)

In shortcut cooking, it is essential to keep your kitchen stocked with the necessary items. So, we've dedicated a whole section to the concept of your meals being pantry-ready!

By having the following items accessible, you will be able to make every recipe in this book (and many other combinations too). You'll always have meals ready and waiting for you. Assemble and serve a nutritious, delicious menu in minutes.

Learn to experiment with different ingredients, substituting and adjusting a personal inventory to develop your own Cookin' Cupboards.

Meet Kathleen: An essential ingredient in the preparation of this cookbook, she transcribed and composed our text under the direction of Graphic Arts Designer, Brad.

CANNED FOODS

Someone else has done the ground work. Convenient canned products (the original "fast food") enable you to retain some control on calories and additives — or whatever you feel is important in your cooking — to give a finished dish your own creative twist.

Can sizes are continually changing. What was a 15 oz. can may now be a 14 ³/₄-oz. can. Buy standard sizes when in doubt.

Artichoke Hearts	**Olives**
Beans	**Tomatoes: Stewed, Sauce**
Chiles	**Vegetables**
Clams	**Water Chestnuts**

ARTICHOKE HEARTS
This delicacy can give a simple salad, pizza, casserole or sandwich an instant gourmet touch. Marinated artichokes **in the jar** contain oil **and** the best taste. Artichoke hearts (and bottoms) **in the can** are water packed and have less fat calories, are less expensive (and less flavorful). But they are a good, healthy alternative when you're watching your fat intake. Jarred or canned? It's your choice.

BEANS
T-N-T = Taste, Nutrition and Texture. They don't call beans the "fuel food" for nothing! Canned or dried, these legumes carry nutritional clout. They are loaded with protein, carbohydrates, fiber and vitamins. (See our "Fiesta Fiasco" chapter.)

•Black Beans are great blended — as a dip for chips or spread for tortillas.

•Kidney Beans make a fine chili filler and hearty addition to many soups. Mash some to thicken a soup. They add protein to tossed salads.

146

•*Garbanzo Beans are good in salads and wonderful in vegetable or Italian soups. Use these (or White Beans) to make hummus.*

•*Refried Beans are already smooth and spiced. This is the most convenient spread (and thickener) yet for anything Mexican — from snacks to soups. There are now nonfat versions. Make sure the label shows no lard or fats.*

CHILES
Chopped or whole, mild green chiles extend color and style to many fast-paced dishes. Layer into casseroles and on grilled sandwiches. Sprinkle over chicken and in ground beef as well as corn.

OLIVES
Keep small cans of sliced, chopped or whole ripe olives in the cupboard. Use in casseroles, salads, baked potatoes and filled tortillas. Canned whole olives are good for quick appetizers and make our "Kitchen Cacciatore" recipe more authentic.

TOMATOES
Canned sauces and tomato preparations (stewed, pureed, diced, salsa, etc.) are worth the investment. Keep lots on hand. The basic canned tomato products usually contain no oil or fat. (Read the label to be sure.)

•*Stewed: Don't stay home without it! Stewed tomatoes are available plain or sea-soned and are essential to making fast salsas, soups, red gravies and sauces.*

•*Sauce: Combine plain tomato sauce or puree with basic spices and/or stewed tomatoes (pureed in processor) or canned soups to make quick homemade sauces, gravies and soups. It will save you money and calories.*

VEGETABLES

When your favorite canned veggies go on sale — stock up. Don't forget to "date and rotate." Never use a bulging or rusted can or one that spurts its contents when opened. If you buy discounted dented cans, avoid those that are dented along the seam. To check the can for safety, squeeze the top and bottom of the can to make sure there is **no** "give." When in doubt, throw it out.

- *Corn, creamed corn: Besides an easy side dish, add it to casseroles, soups and an "all purpose baking mix" to make corn cakes) for flavor, color and crunch.*

- *Roasted Red Peppers: Try to buy a "sweet" pepper variety and avoid the vinegar-packed pepper, which has a tendency to overpower the pepper taste. Use these in cold-cut sandwiches, salads (for color), eggs, meat and poultry casseroles. The dish you're making doesn't have to be Italian to use these sweet ribbons of color. Toss some in your green beans. Of course, they go wonderfully on pizzas but can cross over to Mexican dishes as well.*

- *Yams: These are really sweet potatoes. True yams are something else again — altogether. A good source of vitamins, their ease and convenience of being in the can saves lots of time. A good substitute for fresh. Use as a side dish, layer them into a main dish casserole or sweeten them for dessert. Whip some with nonfat sour cream and seasonings — for color and lots of beta carotene.*

- *Water Chestnuts: Sliced water chestnuts are very mild and will not overpower any dish. They are particularly useful when your recipe has flavor but needs a little crunch. These work in casseroles, salads, even soups.*

DAIRY FOODS

Milk products will separate at too high a heat, so be sure to add the thinner products, like yogurt and sour cream, to less-than-boiling-hot mixtures or at the end of preparation.

Butter/Margarine
Cheese: Cheddar, cream, Monterey Jack, mozzarella, Parmesan
Eggs
Milk
Sour Cream
Yogurt

BUTTER/MARGARINE

It used to be, that's all there was. Now there are various spreads and lite varieties of everything. The drawback to butter is the calories and saturated fat. It's fine if you're using **just a little**. It **is** hard to duplicate the flavor.

Lite and diet margarine contain a higher percentage of water and present problems in moisture levels for baking and create significant spattering in skillet dishes. True margarine gives more predictable results. Your choice.

CHEESE

Possibly nothing beats the rich, satisfying flavor of cheeses. But proceed with caution: This is high-fat territory and some cheeses carry a hefty salt load as well.

Soft and Semisoft Cheeses

•Cream Cheese: Soft and cream textured cheeses help make a sauce rich. If you're going to incorporate cream cheese into a sauce, warm it first in the microwave, for about 30 seconds so it blends more easily.

Consider buying low-fat cream cheese. The flavor is much better than the nonfat and there's usually only a five calorie difference, per two tablespoons, between the reduced and the nonfat versions. Use it where you would sour cream or yogurt but where you want a thicker, creamier effect (without the tang).

Add to mashed potatoes; spread over tortillas, bagels and desserts. Explore the flavored varieties like olive, salmon, strawberry and herb.

•Monterey Jack: Creamy in texture, mild in taste and melts well. It's a great gentle topping useful in almost everything needing cheese — from pizzas to sandwiches.

•Mozzarella: Very, very mild. Stringy when melted. It is naturally lower in fat.

Hard Cheeses

•Sharp Cheddar: When Cheddar cheese is called for, we recommend using sharp or extra sharp. It delivers strong, robust flavor so you may want to reduce the quantity.

Packaged, preshredded Cheddar is convenient (it even comes in resealable bags) but you will pay more. Or stock your freezer with your own preshredded. Just buy a bulk block and "measure up" some resealable plastic bags for future use. Freezing a whole block will compromise texture and consistency, making it unusable as sliced.

Dry Cheese

•Parmesan: very versatile. Add this to almost any dish that needs extra zip. A little goes a long way — with no guilt about fat content!

EGGS

Don't forget the adaptable egg in your scramble to get a meal on the table.

- *In the shell: Good just as they are (cooked of course); they also hold together recipes. Hard boiled eggs are portable and satisfying when you're on the run. Eggs are a good source of protein but contain fat* (an extra large egg has about 80 calories — 45% is fat). Which brings us to ...*

- *Egg substitutes: If you're watching your fat and cholesterol intake, keep egg substitutes pantry-ready. Purchase them in the original frozen form (handy when you run out of real eggs) or liquid form from the dairy section.*

* Fat is contained in the yolk. You can save money **and** fat calories by using only the whites of natural eggs.

MILK

An easy way to cut fat intake is to reach for nonfat, instead of whole or 2%, when a recipe calls for milk. Nonfat milk works the same as whole milk and you can't taste it's nonfat. If you really want the rich texture that whole milk or half and half give, we suggest using CANNED SKIM MILK. It's thick and creamy, and hey — you're not **drinking** it! Plain and simple, nonfat milk is a healthier choice and an easy secret to keep.

- *Sour Cream: A very versatile dairy item. Use the lite version to make a delicious pasta sauce or gravy mixer. It pulls double duty with salad dressings. It's especially good as a base for vegetable sauces. Just a dollop will do! From casseroles to tostadas, it's a perfect addition for Mediterranean to Mexican foods.*

- *Yogurt: Plain or flavored, this milk product can add a different dimension to hot or cold recipes. Try lemon- or orange-flavored yogurt to create a base for a chicken sauce.*

DRY SUPPLIES

Almonds	Bread	Pasta
Beans, dried	Cereal	Rice
Biscuit Mix	Corn Starch	Tortillas

ALMONDS
It is easy to keep nuts on hand. To retain their fresh sweet taste, store in the freezer. Sliced almonds add a quick crunchiness and an interesting flavor to so many recipes — from breakfasts to main dishes to desserts. A little goes a long way. Shake some: They're pretty over salads, poultry sauces and desserts.

BEANS
Let's face it. We know dried beans take more time. Their advantage is their cost-per-quantity. If you are going to cook-ahead-and-freeze for "ready meals," then a large amount at a low price is the way to go.

BISCUIT MIX
An all-purpose baking mix is a must for every pantry. This flour whiz creates casseroles, pancakes and desserts. The lite variety is lower in fat and calories.

BREAD
A staple for life-sustaining meals. Keep it in your freezer to always be ready for that almost instant breakfast, lunch or dinner. (See our "Tons of Buns" chapter.)

BREAD CRUMBS (ITALIAN)
A blend of dry bread and spices that adds volume and taste to casseroles, meat loaf, patties and as a coating for fried or baked foods.

CEREAL
Your cereal of choice can feed you in the morning and coat your fish or chicken at night. Read the nutritional label and look for the grain ingredient (wheat, barley, etc.) to be the **first** listed. (See our "Tons of Buns" chapter.)

CORN STARCH
A good thickening agent for soups gravies, stews and sauces. Follow the box directions.

PASTAS AND RICE
Stretch your dinner dollar and add variety to your recipes using various pastas and rice. Remember, if it takes eight minutes to boil pasta (or twenty to cook rice) then making twice as much will **still** take **only** eight minutes (or twenty minutes). See where we're going with this? Make more than you need and freeze the extra! (See our "Frozen Assets" chapter.)

A time- and space-saving method is to dump cooked pasta or rice (measured to your need) right into a resealable plastic bag. Press out the air. Stores flat. Then with the help of a microwave (or a pot of water — "boiling-bag" style) you'll have a head start on another menu. These easily keep two months frozen.

PASTAS (dry)
Buy only 100% semolina pasta, a heartier product with more body and substance than other types. It will keep its bite when cooked (and even **over**cooked). It won't get mushy when leftovers are reheated. There are many more pastas to choose from than the ones we have listed below. These are our selections for the fast, easy recipes in this book.

Light Weight
- *Angel Hair: This delicate pasta is the winner in the quick-cook category — under five minutes.*
- *Pastina: Tiny but mighty. This smallest of the pastas is perfect for adding to soups or eating with a dab of butter, garlic, Parmesan and red pepper flakes. Add to chicken broth and one beaten egg for a nice "warm your heart" soup. "Little pastas," these are comfort food.*

Middle Weight
- *Linguine: The **only** pasta to serve with our "Italian Clam" sauce. Just the right size: 10" long and $1/8$" wide with texture designed to compliment — the cook.*
- *Spaghetti: An "old stand-by" that keeps on giving. Make your own spaghetti sauce by adding a can of (crushed) stewed tomatoes, tomato sauce and garlic powder. Simple and delicious. (And you can eat it for breakfast!)*

Heavy Weight
- *Fettuccine: The "Alfredo foundation" is a meaty pasta that's usually 10" long and about $1/4$" wide. It will serve a substantial meal and satisfy a hungry eater. It tastes great with lite sour cream and some Parmesan cheese (see our "No Fear Alfredo" recipe.) Add sliced, cooked sausage for that **really** hungry eater.*
- *Radiatore: A meaty, short and squatty pasta with ruffled edges. Great for pasta salads because it envelopes other ingredients. It is also spectacular with sauces. Those little ruffly folds really hold the sauce.*

RICE
An alternative to pasta or an addition to casseroles, stews, soups and side dishes. Remember to cook extra and freeze in serving sizes. Pick types that you prefer.

- *Brown: Has a nutty flavor, is chewier to eat and is more nutritious than the plain.*

•*Plain/Converted: Most commonly used and widely accepted.*

•*Seasoned Mixes: When adding rice to soups, try a flavored blend. Although the mixes generally aren't any faster cooking, they do reduce the time it would take to measure, add and adjust seasonings. Can be high in **sodium** and **fat**.*

TORTILLAS (and Tortilla Chips):
There are choices in tortillas: corn, white corn, whole and sprouted wheat. Read the label. These products often contain fats. Avoid those containing lard or cottonseed oil.

FROZEN FOODS
Frozen is almost as healthy as fresh and far more recipe-ready (no washing or waste). Keep our book's ingredients (as well as your favorites) in your coldest cupboard.

Berries (see SWEETS)
Bread Dough
Chicken Breasts
Vegetables: broccoli, carrots, corn, onion, peas, Southwest salad, spinach

BERRIES *(see SWEETS)*

BREAD DOUGH
This frozen but very flexible "staff of life" is a **real** shortcut to down-home taste. Simply microwave to defrost (follow package directions) and use as pizza base, biscuits or "homemade" bread. Look for a brand that is low in fat — delicious! The smell alone is worth the price.

CHICKEN BREASTS

Bulk frozen breasts belong in your freezer-ready food group. They are a "must have." Buy them bagged. Bake them (right from the frozen state) at high heat (500° for 15 minutes) and you'll have tender, juicy chicken ready in no time. Great sliced for grilled sandwiches, stripped for salads or chunked for soups. Other options: barbecue, broil, fry or microwave.

VEGETABLES

There's simply no excuse these days not to have some of your Five-A-Days on ice. For adding to casseroles, soups, even salads, there's no faster way to mix and match for your homemade fast food. Use right from the frozen state or quick-thaw in the microwave or under cool, running water.

- *Broccoli: Whole "trees" or chopped? Boxed or bagged? This cabbage-cousin adds a big boost of flavor and color. Good in casseroles and rice dishes.*

- *Peppers: Look for bags of assorted sweet peppers. These are a money-saving investment compared to imported fresh yellow and orange beauties. A great way to add a splash of color to casseroles, stir fry. They become limp when thawed so use in cooked foods.*

- *Spinach: After thawing, drain well. Whether you prefer the chopped or whole leaf — you should squ-e-e-z-e it dry. Then add it to soups, dips, or make it a hot side dish with a scoop of light sour cream and some dry onion soup mix.*

•Onion: Cry at the thought of slicing or chopping onions? There are frozen, chopped onions in the freezer section! Use these next time you want onion in a hot side dish (when thawed, they become limp, so we don't recommend them for fresh preparations).

•Carrots: Always available, these are packed with Vitamin A. Seasoned right, **even** the kids will eat them. Colorful and nutritious addition to casseroles and green salads.

•Corn: Petite white or standard yellow corn can add so much goodness and flavor to a dish. Include corn in your casseroles, salads and side dishes. You can even put some in your blender when making pancake batter and have presto-corn-cakes.

•Peas: Quick color. Bang the bag on the floor to separate the frozen peas, then sprinkle over salads. By the time you fix another dish, they're thawed! They complement almost any soup or casserole and can be added to "No Fear Alfredo." (See our "Fasta Pasta" chapter.)

•Southwest Salad: A handy toss-in for pastas, stews and casseroles of all kinds. Its medley of vegetables and beans make spontaneous put-togethers a breeze.

ORANGE JUICE
This should be on everyone's grocery list and in everyone's freezer. A good source of Vitamin C that can be used in many ways, from a nutritious beverage to start your day, to a flavor enhancer for salad dressings and chicken and meat sauces.

MEATS, POULTRY AND SEAFOOD

Whether you let the supermarket do your cooking or you buy to cook ahead to stock your freezer; use these shortcuts with meat to reduce your kitchen time.

BEEF

You can find a nutritious bargain in beef. An occasional steak or burger can taste **so** good and doesn't take a lot of time to prepare. If you're counting calories (or cholesterol), buy leaner cuts of beef. When in doubt, ask your butcher.

Instead of buying prepackaged ground beef, select a package (or more when on sale) of lean stew meat and have the butcher triple-grind it. This can be even less expensive than "case" ground beef (which **can** contain more fat).

We recommend making meat balls from lean ground beef and seasonings (and perhaps some sausage). Cook and keep ready to use in your freezer. It will give you a swift solution to a mealtime-madness moment.

Precook meat balls, cool and put into resealable plastic bags in serving portions. Your meat is ready to be reheated for pasta or rice dishes, crumbled in tortillas or layered in a sandwich.

CHICKEN

You can't go wrong with the "original white meat."

• *Fresh: Skinless, boneless packs from the meat case saves prep **and** cleanup time (if you can afford them). Cook them like a steak (you probably paid as much!). To check for doneness, pierce meat with a fork. The juices should run clear if it has finished cooking.*

•*Frozen: (See FROZEN FOODS.) A "must have" item.*

•*Precooked: Already baked (or rotisserie) whole, deli chicken is the ultimate in convenience. (See our chapter "Chicken On The Run.") They keep about three days in the refrigerator. Remove the skin to save on fat calories.*

COLD CUTS
These may have a limited refrigerator life but they prove to be a handy option for many meals: lean turkey, ham or chicken. It can be the answer to a meal-on-the-run or a snack attack. Available in low-sodium and fat.

TURKEY
•*Breast only: Buy a two-pound, bone-in portion. Season with poultry spices. Bake at 500° for thirty minutes. Slice and serve with gravy for a quick traditional meal. Just like the real thing, good for sandwich slices too.*

•*Ground turkey: (white + dark meat) can be a good substitute for ground beef in recipes. Use it as you would ground round. Or buy "white meat only."*

•*Turkey Tenderloins: Boneless turkey breast sautés quickly. Try coating with egg white then dipping in Italian bread crumbs. Season with salt and garlic powder. Fry each side three to five minutes.*

PORK
The tenderloin is one of our favorite cuts. It's pricy but there is no waste. It is delicious and simple to prepare. They come vacuum-sealed and will keep for a limited time in the refrigerator (or longer in the freezer). Grill it on the barbecue or bake in oven using a high heat. Delicious with plum sauce (try the jarred baby food — it's less expensive.)

SAUSAGE
There are now some exotically delectable (and lean) sausages. Buy the precooked types; grind them up to mix with other ground meats (turkey is good) for a super burger, pizza topping or tortilla filler. Slice and add them to a white sauce and serve over pasta for a fabulous effect. If you really want to keep it simple, just heat and serve with a sauce. (See SOUPS, SAUCES AND SPREADS section, this appendix.)

SEAFOOD

Bay Shrimp	Imitation Crab
Clams	Tuna

BAY SHRIMP
Precooked, ready to add to pastas, salads, tortillas, appetizer, toppings, stuffed avocados and tomatoes. If reheated, flavor becomes **strong**.

CLAMS
A mild seafood taste and distinctly chewy texture. Try something different! How about canned clams as a pizza topping? "Beef up" a can of clam chowder soup with an extra can of clams and a squirt of Worcestershire sauce. You can toss them in red **or** white sauce to serve over pasta.

IMITATION CRAB
White Pollock fish is seasoned with (very little) real crab juice and spices. It doesn't taste like the real thing but is a fine crab substitute for sandwiches, spreads, casseroles and dips.

TUNA

Water-packed albacore is your best bet for tuna: value and flavor. Add to casseroles and sandwiches. Select "dolphin-safe" brands. Always keep available for a quick lunch or dinner salad.

PRODUCE

You will need perishables on your shopping list to round out your recipes and balance your daily diet. Some things are just better (more flavorful or more finely textured) when fresh. Many have good cold storage life.

 Remember to visit your local farmers' market for a great selection of produce.

LETTUCE

It now comes to the table a **lot** easier. No more washing, drying and shredding. It's available already clean and chopped, prebagged, in the produce department. Many stores offer blends of lettuce for specific types of salad (and even the dressing and croutons right in the package). Convenient, yes, and a bit pricy. Remember, the darker the leaf, the more vitamins. (See our chapter "Fire-Crackin' Salads.")

- *Romaine: Hardy, dark green leaves make a super Caesar salad.*
- *Butter: Soft, very delicate flavor — sweet. Very popular.*
- *Red Leaf: stronger taste and very colorful.*
- *Spinach: Don't forget spinach for salads. It makes a great alternative. Try this quick salad: bagged spinach leaves, presliced, packaged mushrooms, tossed with low-fat bacon pieces in a vinaigrette dressing — a "Two-Minute Wonder" salad!*

Green Onions

A good green sprinkle can color-up just about any mealtime entreé. Tastes great too. Chop up the long green ends and get wild.

Cilantro

Don't be without this fabulous herb. It's a must for any South of the Border or Far East menu. It is also fantastic in tossed green or even fruit salads.

Parsley

This old stand-by is not just for garnish anymore. Try actually eating it. Dress up a salad or sprinkle onto mashed potatoes to create a fancy plate. It is a must in "Lisa's Italian Dressing" (see "Sauces" appendix for recipe), a terrific marinade over crab, cooked meats or freshly sliced tomatoes.

FRUIT

If you buy fruit in season, you'll pay **less** and chances are the **quality** will be better. Our stand-by favorites include fruits that are good for snacking **and** cooking.

- *Granny Smith Apples: The tartness and firmness of these apples make it possible to stuff a turkey or a pie, add a cold crisp sweetness to a salad, or simply divide their bounty into sections for snacking.*

- *Apricots, Peaches and Pineapples: These fruits can be found fresh, frozen or canned and have many uses. Put them in your yogurt or on pancakes. Snack on them whole, halved or chunked in your lunch (or in between). Add color, sweetness and texture to beef, poultry and ham dishes to give them a subtle suggestion of exotic fruitiness. Desserts are easy with these ingredients at your command. If you enjoy a glass of wine, you'll enjoy it more with a sweet slice of fresh peach or apricot in the glass.*

- *Oranges: Sliced for snacking, floating in hot apple cider or garnishing a side dish. Squeeze its juice to add a fresh twang to sauces. Grate its peel to give zest to anything you want!*

POTATOES
Fresh is best. With microwaves, there's little excuse **not** to use fresh. We don't recommend you freeze cooked (or even refrigerate fresh) potatoes. It's a texture thing. (See October's chapter, "This Spud's for You," and "Keeping an Eye on Potatoes.") When not even a microwave is fast enough, make whipped, mashed potatoes in under five minutes by using a boxed potato variety (made from 100% potato flakes). Use nonfat milk instead of water and add a little butter or margarine. Potato flakes are also great for adding body to a meat loaf or thickening casseroles, sauces or soups.

TOMATOES
These round bursts of sunshine are so good **IF** they taste like a tomato. Try purchasing them at a farmers' market or grow your own. Just don't pay high prices for something that tastes like — nothing! (See "Yumm-atoes" in our August chapter.) Coat them with Italian dressing. Chop for salads and salsas. Slice to garnish a dish or sandwich. Or, stuff some for a fancy side dish.

MUSHROOMS
Fresh, this edible fungus can grace a pizza, give depth to a sauce, be grilled for a sandwich, accompany eggs, or add interest to a vegetable side dish. Most stores now

carry more than just the white, button variety. Experiment! Try a fungus new to you. Each variety has its own characteristics. Ask the produce clerk for assistance.

- *Presliced, packaged mushrooms: a little less nutritious, a bit more expensive — but a **great** shortcut.*

- *Canned/jarred: You pay twice as much for canned mushrooms, ounce per ounce, but it's a good idea to keep some for a mushroom emergency.*

ONIONS

Chop, slice, or puree your way to a speedy, savory meal with one of the many varieties this sassy bulb has to offer. There are a thousand (or more) recipes that require an onion. And to be sure, the onion has quite a success record. Sautéing onions (caramelizing) before adding them to recipes, helps bring out their flavor. Even if you don't like to eat onions, try mincing or pureeing a sweet one and adding just a **little** to your recipe, for a subtle touch.

- *Green: Add color, flavor and texture to all kinds of dishes with a simple sprinkle from its green leaves.*

- *Frozen: a "no tear" version for casseroles, sautéing or soups.*

- *Rustic: white, yellow, red and Bermuda all have strong, tangy flavors.*

- *Sweet: Maui, Walla Walla and Vidalia. They are sweet, juicy and not sharp in taste. But watch those prices. If they are too expensive, take a shortcut — sweeten an onion with a $1/2$ teaspoon of sugar when sautéing. Shorter shelf life.*

SEASONINGS AND SWEETENERS

These flavor-enhancers are very versatile and necessary in shortcut cooking.

🍴 *Buy spices in small quantities and keep no longer than six months. Higher quality brands deliver more impact.*

Bacon	Corn Syrup	Hot Red Pepper Sauce	Sugar: White, Brown
Bread Crumbs	Curry Powder	Italian Dressing (dry)	Sweet Hot Mustard
Capers	Dill Weed	Italian Herb Seasoning	Vinegar
Cayenne	Garlic Pepper	Onion Soup Mix	Worcestershire
Chili Powder	Garlic Powder	Salt and Pepper	Sauce
Cinnamon	Honey	Sherry	

BACON PIECES
Now available in low-fat! These little morsels pack a load of flavor. A small amount goes a long way. Liven up vegetable dishes, salads, egg recipes, pizzas, potatoes — with a sprinkle of bacon pieces.

BREAD CRUMBS (ITALIAN)
A blend of dry bread, herbs and spices that adds volume and taste to casseroles, meat loaf, meat balls, patties. Also use as a coating for fried or baked foods.

CAPERS
Provide instant bursts of flavor, color and style. Use over chicken breasts, fish, tomatoes or on bagels with cream cheese. Caution: These are salty!

CAYENNE
Use this chili pepper sparingly. Really adds the kick to foods you want to spice up.

CHILI POWDER
A "must have" for that Southwestern effect. This strong mixture is actually a blend of several spices and seasonings. Look for specialty choices like zesty or hot.

CINNAMON
Add to French toast, white pasta sauces, rice (for a Middle Eastern effect) or to flavor coffee, apple cider or apple sauce.

CORN SYRUP
Light or dark, this thick sweetener can moisturize like honey but has pantry staying power — no crystallizing problem. Try a half-measure when dressings call for sugar.

CURRY POWDER
Gives a Middle Eastern flair to ordinary dishes like rice, vegetables, meats, sauces. Use sparingly. Curry can range from mild to hot blends.

DILL WEED
Fresh is very different than dried yet both have interesting characteristics. Use with sauces, potatoes, green salads and fish.

GARLIC PEPPER
This is one pepper that can spark up any dish; a marriage of black pepper and garlic. A **hearty** combination.

GARLIC POWDER
"Gotta have it!" The majority of recipes in this book call for garlic powder. (Lisa is often heard chanting, "I can't live without my garlic powder.")

HONEY
Use anywhere you would use sugar. Because you're adding moisture you will need to adjust liquids. (Honey is not recommended for very young children.)

HOT RED PEPPER SAUCE
Hot and spicy, a little **dash** will "do ya." Great on almost anything for extra pizazz.

ITALIAN DRESSING MIX (dry)
Sprinkle on dry — this all-in-one packet of multiple flavors will dress up chicken, pizza, and bean salad. It can be mixed in regular barbecue sauce.

ITALIAN HERB SEASONINGS
This multi-blend of dried oregano, basil, thyme (and others) turn ordinary tomato sauce into a ready-to-serve pizza spread or pasta sauce. Zip up zucchini with a dash. Watch this spicy Italian; it's known to have a bite to it.

ONION SOUP MIX (dry)
This powerful packet of dried onion and spices makes good dips better — mixed with lite sour cream. Super in meat loaves or sprinkled in casseroles for a quick flavor fix.

SALT AND PEPPER
We don't salt and pepper many of our dishes. We leave it to your discretion. Sprinkle pepper to your heart's content, just don't shake that salt too hard.

SHERRY
Buy regular cream sherry. Avoid cooking sherry as it is high in sodium (**and** you can't **drink** it). Gives dishes a distinct taste that goes well with imitation crab, scrambled eggs, sauces and stews.

SUGAR
White, Brown: A spoonful helps liven up sauces, dressings, desserts, vegetables, even onions.

SWEET HOT MUSTARD
It's like gold. Don't be without it! Use it as your secret ingredient in everything from salad dressings to casseroles. Some brands contain oil but, for the flavor it imparts, it is worth the calories.

VINEGAR
Oak vinegar is hearty, has less acidity than balsamic, and is stronger in color and flavor. Fine additive for most salads and dressings. Sprinkle a little over lamb or beef. Softens the 'gamey' flavor and is a natural meat tenderizer.

WORCESTERSHIRE SAUCE
This anchovy based (!) sauce can sneak into all kinds of dishes, giving them an added boost by harmonizing flavors.

SOUPS, SAUCES AND SPREADS:
A quick fix, soups of all kind can be the start of something delicious. Keep a variety of these treasures handy to baste, blend, toss, sprinkle, stir or coat.

SOUPS
Canned Broths: Beef, Chicken, Vegetable
Creamed Soups: Chicken, Mushroom, Clam Chowder

CANNED BROTH
A very convenient ingredient for building more complex soups, and making sauces and gravies. Try purchasing the newer varieties of low-sodium or low-fat.

•Beef: This broth has a full, robust taste with lots of flavor. (Having this on hand makes it easy to sauté some onions for a quick onion soup.)

•Chicken: This liquid gold is a real time saver. It is such a simple flavor booster. You no longer have to boil whole chickens to extract this rich taste. Super as a substitute for water (in rice dishes) or milk (in potato recipes). It is also an excellent sauce and gravy base. Saves time and calories. Remove any hard, white particles from the surface of the broth while in the can (this is fat).

•Vegetable: Use it, as you would chicken or beef broth, to add flavor without adding fat. Some have a distinct (rather strong) onion flavor. Experiment so that it does not overpower other ingredients in your recipe.

CREAMED SOUPS (condensed or concentrated soups)
Instead of the classic roux (made with butter and flour), just open a can of low-fat cream soup. ALSO wonderful for making pasta sauces. We recommend condensed, Italian tomato style but if you cannot find it, do the following: To one can of regular tomato soup add two tablespoons of Italian dry herbs, one tablespoon of garlic powder.

Mix and match soups (even two or three) for extra flavor. Add garlic powder, curry, ginger, etc., to creamed soups.

Most low-fat soups have less flavor, so always remember to spice them up with your personal favorite seasonings.

SAUCES and SPREADS

The right sauce or spread will help harmonize (and moisturize) your creation.

Barbecue Sauce	**Horseradish**	**Mayonnaise**
Chili Sauce	**Ketchup**	**Pickle Relishes**

- *Barbecue Sauce: Not just for the barbecue. Try it on sandwiches, pizza, burgers and sausages. Drizzle over deli-cooked chicken.*

- *Chili Sauce: It's ketchup with a zip! Try it in meat loaf, creamy salad dressings or serve with seafood.*

- *Horseradish: Another secret enhancer. Use it straight or to dress up recipes. Creamy is the best choice because it **doesn't** contain fat. Makes a great beef sauce when blended with lite sour cream (see "Beefy Cover-Up" in "The Great Cover-Ups: Sauces and Dressings," Appendix B).*

- *Ketchup: Blend in salad dressings, add to ground beef, or use as a spread. Look for spicy varieties.*

- *Mayonnaise (and its spiced-up cousins): This dress-up-your-sandwich-and-salad spread/dressing can vary in fat, taste and price. Remember to read that label to determine fat content. Light and low-fat are very different in flavor and calories. The nonfat still doesn't cut the mustard for flavor — yet. It can be bland. Use it to carry other flavorful spices — drizzle it over veggies. Mix it with sweet hot mustard for a tasty sandwich spread.*

- *Pickle Relishes: A red pickle relish makes a spicy fish sauce when added to lite mayo and diced red onion. A real perk.*

SWEETS

*There are many ways to satisfy your sweet tooth. Some are even fancy enough for guests. Stock these components for quick combinations (if your sweet tooth is in control). Stock this list for the occasional "snack attack." Don't deprive yourself of a treat **once** in a while.*

Cake Mix	Fudge Topping	Marshmallow Creme	Powdered Sugar
Cookies	Ice Cream	Oatmeal	
Frozen Fruit	Jams	Pound Cake	

CAKE MIX
Keep a ready-made dry mix in the cupboard for a fast dessert. A speedy topping can also be made. (See "No-Sweat Sweets.")

COOKIES
Besides a harmless little nibble now and then, you can crumble these (low-fat varieties) in the food processor, to give a crunchy topping to fruit or ice creams or to line a pie plate for a fast crust.

FROZEN FRUIT
From breakfast to dessert, frozen fruit offers a light and nutritious ingredient palette.

•Peaches: Presliced, these offer a calorie savings over the syrup-laden, canned varieties and often show more color. You may need to sweeten a bit.

•Berries: No matter what your favorite is, be sure to keep some of these icy jewels on hand. Again, the individually frozen straw-, black-, boysen- or blue- berries offer a rainbow of flavors and interest for everything to breakfast yogurt-toppings to fancy after-dinner treats.

FUDGE TOPPING

A real gooey treat, this no-fat, dark, creamy chocolate is the perfect finish for low-fat ice cream. It contains no cocoa butter — but does have lots of calories. Use for an occasional treat with most desserts, as a dip for fruits or frosting for a simple cake.

ICE CREAM

Tastes so good! If you are concerned about the fat content, try a variation like nonfat yogurt, reduced fat ice cream, sherbets or ice milk.

JAMS

Make good flavor-enhancers. Besides the ordinary spread for your bread, it's a nice insert for cakes. An innovative sweetener for salad dressings.

MARSHMALLOW CREME

Sticky spread with lots of sweet taste. It seems to be making a comeback to modern kitchens. This white sweetie can top a graham cracker or be used as a cake filling.

OATMEAL

Add texture and nutrition (and crunch) to your dessert topping. (See our chapter "No-Sweat Sweets.")

POUND CAKE

Plain — but not for long with the addition of some of these other ingredients, like jams, marshmallow creme or fudge topping. Keep one frozen for a last-minute indulgence.

POWDERED SUGAR

Give visual appeal to desserts. An easy cover-up for a store-bought cake: place shapes of paper (like circles) over the top of a plain cake and dust with sugar. Looks great.

MISCELLANEOUS

OILS
They ease our preparation and add flavors. Try some gourmet infused oils. Mostly olive, they are instilled with the essence of herbs, chiles, etc.

Olive: There is quite a variety of this tree-ripened extract.

- *Extra-virgin: It is the first press of the olive and contains about 1% acid. It does have a strong, robust flavor and may be overbearing in some dishes.*

- *Regular: This is usually a combination of refined olive oil and virgin.*

- *Light: This only means it is lighter in color and fragrance. It is a good oil for frying as it doesn't burn easily.*

NONSTICK SPRAYS (COATINGS) *for sautéing, baking and broiling*
They are often made of corn oil but we recommend an olive oil-based one. Spray whenever you don't want food to stick. Spray the barbecue grill!

REMEMBER

Buy low-fat and low-sodium products when appropriate.

Recycle glass and bi-metal cans (if available in your area).

Products that are over packaged usually mean they're overpriced (and not good for the environment).

Sauces and Dressings

*Having these in your bag of tricks can **speed** recipe preparations and add **variety** to busy weekday meals. Some can do double duty equally well hot or cold. Others can even make a triple play, from fish to fowl to meats. You can easily "create and refrigerate" many for continued use as their need arises.*

Try the same sauce over pasta and potatoes, not just rice. Move a dressing from the lettuce category to the fruit salad domain or the reverse. If you like a cold dressing (like "Blue Cheese Blast"), try it as a sauce over hot vegetables.

*You get the idea. Get the **most** mileage out of these versatile cover-alls.*

SAUCES

ALFREDO SAUCE (from "No Fear Alfredo")

8 oz.	lite sour cream
6 oz.	lite cream cheese
1 $^1/_2$ Tbs.	sugar
$^1/_2$ tsp.	nutmeg
$^1/_4$ cup	Parmesan cheese

In medium, nonstick saucepan, add all ingredients. Heat until blended. Stir often to avoid sauce sticking to bottom of pan. Pour over cooked pasta.

ARTICHOKE SAUCE

$^1/_4$ cup	low-fat mayonnaise
2 Tbs.	sesame oil
1 Tbs.	sugar
1 tsp.	vinegar
$^1/_2$ tsp.	lemon juice

Blend all the above. Serve cold. Super dipping sauce for artichokes!

BAR-B-QUE SAUCE, WOW-EE!

4 tsp.	ketchup
2 tsp.	red wine vinegar
2 tsp.	honey
1 tsp.	chili powder
1 tsp.	garlic powder

In a small bowl, mix all ingredients. Microwave for 1 minute or until hot — blends flavors.

BEEFY COVER-UP SAUCE

$1/4$ cup	lite sour cream
2 Tbs.	creamy horseradish

Stir well to blend. Serve with most beef dishes.

CREAM SAUCE

3 Tbs.	butter
1	sweet onion, diced
3 Tbs.	flour
2 cups	nonfat milk
10 $^3/_4$ oz.	can cream of celery soup (98% fat free)
13 $^3/_4$ oz.	can hearts of artichoke (water packed), minced
$^1/_2$ cup	Cheddar cheese, shredded
1 tsp.	garlic pepper

In a saucepan over medium heat, sauté chopped onion in melted butter until translucent. Add flour and stir. Gradually pour in milk, blending thoroughly. Keep stirring while it thickens. Dump in the celery soup, minced artichoke hearts, shredded cheese and garlic pepper. Mix well and let it cook another 5 minutes (keep stirring!).

CROSS DRESSING
Excellent hot or cold.

1 cup	lite mayonnaise
$^1/_4$ cup	sugar
3 Tbs.	red wine vinegar
1 tsp.	curry powder

Mix ingredients well. Add creamy marinade to such vegetables as broccoli and carrots.

FIVE-MINUTE PASTA SAUCE

14 oz.	can tomato bisque soup
$1/2$ cup	lite sour cream
2 Tbs.	garlic powder
	Parmesan cheese to taste

Mix soup with sour cream and garlic. Heat in microwave and serve over hot pasta.

HURRY HULA SAUCE

$1/2$ cup	pineapple juice
$1 1/2$ tsp.	corn starch
2 Tbs.	lite soy sauce
2 Tbs.	honey
1 Tbs.	vinegar

Mix corn starch in pineapple juice and stir until well blended. Add all other ingredients. Microwave on high for 2 minutes or until thickened.

HURRIED CURRY SAUCE

10 ¼ oz.   can low-fat mushroom soup
2 Tbs.   curry powder
2 Tbs.   garlic powder

Heat in sauce pan or microwave for two minutes until flavors blend. Serve with many different recipes in this book. Ideal with chicken, pork or even veggies.

MEAT MARINADE

¼ cup   soy sauce
2 Tbs.   chile oil
2 Tbs.   red-wine vinegar
1 Tbs.   chili powder
1 Tbs.   sugar
1 Tbs.   garlic powder

Mix well. This is a wonderful marinade for pork.

PACIFIC RIM SAUCE

$^1/_3$ cup	sherry
1 tsp.	corn starch
3 Tbs.	lite soy sauce
3 Tbs.	honey
1 tsp.	chicken bouillon, dissolved
1 tsp.	lemon juice
1 tsp.	ground ginger
1 Tbs.	garlic powder

In medium microwaveable bowl, mix sherry with corn starch to blend. Add rest of ingredients. Microwave for about 2 minutes until slightly thickened. Cool and serve as dipping sauce. Or use as a marinade.

PORK OF MY HEART SAUCE

4 oz.	jar plums (in baby food section of the supermarket)
1 Tbs.	brown sugar

In microwaveable bowl, add the above and microwave for 45 seconds. Great with pork or chicken. Good sandwich spread.

SASSY SALSA

2	15-oz. cans stewed tomatoes
1	bunch cilantro, wash and remove stems
$1/4$	bunch parsley (optional)
1	small red onion, peeled
$1^1/_2$ Tbs.	chili powder
$1^1/_2$ Tbs.	garlic powder
$1/_2$ tsp.	cayenne pepper (up to $1^1/_2$ tsp. = hot)
$1/_2$ tsp.	lemon juice
$1/_2$ tsp.	sugar (up to $1^1/_2$ tsp. = sweet)

Add stewed tomatoes first, then the cilantro and seasonings, to blender. Chop in blender for approximately 30 seconds, until mixed. Pour into a one-quart glass jar. Refrigerate.

SMARTER TARTAR

$1/_2$ cup	lite sour cream
3 Tbs.	dill weed
1 Tbs.	low-fat mayonnaise
$1/_2$ tsp.	sugar
6	drops lemon juice (plastic "squeeze")

In small bowl, mix all ingredients. Great complement to fish. Super substitute for high-fat tartar sauce.

SWEET 'N' SOUR SAUCE

$1/2$ cup	orange juice
1 tsp.	corn starch
$1/2$ Tbs.	honey or corn syrup
1 tsp.	vinegar
$1/2$ tsp.	nutmeg

In a small bowl, mix orange juice with corn starch. Stir well. Add vinegar, corn syrup and nutmeg. Cover and microwave on high for 1 minute 45 seconds. Stir well. Let cool and pour over vegetables, rice or meats.

"TO THAI FOR" SAUCE

8 oz.	can crushed pineapple, drained
1 Tbs.	sweet hot mustard
1 Tbs.	honey
1 tsp.	garlic powder
$1/2$ tsp.	ground ginger
$1/2$ tsp.	chili powder

In small bowl, mix all ingredients to blend flavors. Heat and serve with your favorite rice or poultry.

TEN-MINUTE PASTA SAUCE

2	15-oz. cans stewed tomatoes
8 oz.	canned tomato sauce
8 oz.	package fresh mushrooms, sliced
2 Tbs.	Italian dried herb seasonings
2 Tbs.	garlic powder
1 Tbs.	gravy 'browning' sauce

Heat all ingredients in medium saucepan (or microwave in a bowl 6 minutes on high). Serve with hot pasta.

TERIYAKI DIPPING SAUCE

$1/4$ cup	lite soy sauce
$1/8$ cup	sherry
3 Tbs.	honey
2 Tbs.	garlic powder
1 tsp.	ground ginger
1 tsp.	lemon juice

Mix all in microwaveable bowl. Heat for 2 minutes. If you want a thicker sauce, add one teaspoon of corn starch (dissolve in a little **cool** water first) to mixture. Stir well. Microwave again for another minute or until sauce thickens. Let cool. A super recipe to use as a marinade or dipping sauce for meats.

VEGGIE MARINADE

8 oz.	canned tomato sauce
$^{1}/_{4}$ cup	vinegar
$^{1}/_{4}$ cup	olive oil
1 Tbs.	sugar
1 tsp.	dry mustard (or 1 Tbs. sweet hot mustard)
1 tsp.	Worcestershire sauce

In small mixing bowl, stir all ingredients until well blended. Use this multi-purpose marinade on meat or cooked vegetables.

WHAM LAMB SAUCE

$^{1}/_{2}$ cup	mint jelly
$^{1}/_{4}$ cup	lime juice
$^{3}/_{4}$ cup	honey

Stir together all ingredients. Serve at room temperature. Perfect for any lamb dish.

DRESSINGS

BLUE CHEESE BLAST

1 cup	low-fat mayonnaise
4 oz.	crumbled blue cheese
1$^1/_2$ Tbs.	Worcestershire sauce
1 Tbs.	garlic powder
$^1/_2$ tsp.	sugar

Add all ingredients to a blender. Mix well. Refrigerate. Keeps about 2 weeks. Great baguette spread. Top your veggies or salads.

CROSS DRESSING
(See page 178.)

LISA'S ITALIAN DRESSING

1 cup	fresh parsley, no stems
5	garlic cloves
1¹/₂ tsp.	sugar
¹/₄ cup	olive oil
3 Tbs.	balsamic vinegar

In miniprocessor, mix parsley and garlic well. Place in small container. Top with salt, olive oil vinegar and sugar. Shake well. Refrigerate. To serve, bring to room temperature. Using a fork, serve up parsley so most of the marinade stays behind. Place on freshly cut summer tomatoes or on sliced rounds of French bread.

MEDITERRANEAN DRESSING

¹/₄ cup	low-fat mayonnaise
2 Tbs.	garlic powder
1 tsp.	curry powder
1 tsp.	sugar
¹/₂ tsp.	allspice

In small bowl, add all ingredients. To thin dressing, add 2 Tbs. water. Serve with salad, veggies or chicken dish.

MEXICAN DRESSING

11 oz.	can Mexican-style stewed tomatoes
2 Tbs.	garlic powder
1 Tbs.	chili powder
1 tsp.	sugar

Mix all ingredients in a blender. Avoid leaving any big chunks of tomato. Serve over your favorite lettuce. Wonderful with avocado. Add crushed tortilla chips to a salad for extra crunch.

ORIENTAL DRESSING

$^1/_4$ cup	lite soy sauce
1 Tbs.	brown sugar
1 tsp.	garlic powder
$^1/_2$ tsp.	ground ginger
$^1/_2$ tsp.	lemon juice
2 Tbs.	sesame seeds
2 Tbs.	olive oil

In a small microwaveable bowl, stir ingredients to dissolve sugar. Microwave 1 minute on high to blend flavors. Let cool and serve over salad.

SWEET HOT MUSTARD DRESSING

1 pkg.   dry Italian salad dressing mix
1 tsp.   sweet hot mustard
1 tsp.   honey

Make your dressing as directed on the package, except use olive oil. Use balsamic vinegar, or if you can find it, oak-aged vinegar. Then add mustard and honey. Shake and serve. It's so good!

2001 ISLAND DRESSING

$^1/_2$ cup   low-fat mayonnaise
$^1/_4$ cup   chili sauce
2 tsp.   red pickle relish
$^1/_2$ tsp.   hot red pepper sauce

Mix all ingredients. This is a super, low-fat salad dressing. Perfect for shrimp or crab salads or delicious on a salad of just tomatoes.

ROBUST RED RELISH

$^1/_4$ cup   red currant jelly
2 Tbs.   vinegar
1 tsp.   honey

In small microwaveable bowl, heat 30 seconds to blend flavors. Great with pork.

Survival Tips, Tools and Tidbits

ShortCuts from start to finish, that's what you need to take the easy way out of the kitchen.

 **Planning Meals**

 **Shopping Tips**

 **Maintaining Mix and Match Provisions**

 **Preparation ShortCuts**

 **Storing Ready-Meals — Your Freezer, Your Friend**

 **Reducing Cleanup**

Have you lost your zest for cooking? Does it take too long? Do the clerks at the "take-out" window know you on a first-name basis? Then maybe you're ready to try some shortcuts. Rethink some of your old methods and add some fresh techniques!

This section will help you ease your way back into — and then out of — the kitchen again and again. Take control of your time and money.

Follow these tips from the pages of our book and you will soon be on your way. Remember: If you have to do something three times a day, make it **FUN**, *FAST* and **HEALTHY**!

Planning Meals
Planning ahead can help you manage your time and nutrition.

Make foods in advance, then microwave your mealtimes. When preparing meals, make twice the amount you'll need. Freeze for another day. This will definitely reduce the frequency of dinnertime panic attacks.

For pasta dishes, use vermicelli or angel hair, which cook up in under four minutes. You'll be ready to use that extra pasta, frozen in a resealable plastic bag. Simply thaw and heat up in your microwave right in the bag.

Plan on flavor but not fat: Readily available, fresh-cut herbs like cilantro, parsley, watercress, tarragon thyme or basil will add a quick zip to salads (and many other dishes). But, use sparingly. They can pack a punch! Want convenience? Try growing herbs in your garden. It's easy!

Speaking of salads, bacon is a frequently requested add-in flavor. Jarred pieces are available with less fat. Now you can put the flavor back in some of those family favorites.

Need a dependable vegetable? Broccoli is always available (even frozen) and inexpensive for its nutritional value. This high-fiber green can be eaten cooked or raw. Peel the stems of fresh broccoli and add them to salads for a great crunch.

Make a point of using up any extras. For example, if you're hollowing out tomatoes to stuff for dinner, save the innards for your next meal, like an egg scramble or a pasta sauce.

Try duplicating your "take-out" pizza orders at home. Select one of the already cooked versions of pizza crust or "make and bake your own" using frozen bread dough. (Don't use the tube-type refrigerator rolls for pizza crust. They don't turn out as well and often have more fat.) Frozen loaves of dough save you just that, dough **and** calories.

If you use a jarred pizza sauce, read the label for fat content. It may contain oil. It can take 8 to 12 ounces to cover one crust — a lot of extra calories! Try our quick pasta sauce recipes instead.

For salads, casseroles or sautés, plan on interesting ingredients to give variety, like water chestnuts, roasted red peppers or artichoke hearts. They can be pricy but make home meals more like eating out. Try to find water-packed products. Reduce the fat calories of oil-processed foods by draining then rinsing in cool running water.

Think turkey for a large group or a holiday dinner. Count on leftovers if you cook the whole bird. Count on saving time if you purchase and cook only the part your family likes. A turkey breast cooks a lot faster than an entire bird, and white meat is low in fat.

Save the stock from chicken or turkey (or use canned broth) to sauté in instead of butter or margarine. You can then budget your calories for — dessert!

When planning a meal using ground turkey, use breast meat. Watch supermarket ground turkey! It might contain dark meat (and by law, even skin). Buy breast meat. It is low (about 1%, by weight) in fat. White meat can be bland. Spice it up!

Avoid potential dangers of bacteria multiplying in poultry and stuffing by not stuffing the bird in advance. You can still stuff. But you may even make the stuffing a day in advance. Refrigerate it right in its bowl. Cook it separately or double the batch and have stuffing enough for all the leftovers. Don't wait for a holiday to make stuffing! It's a great way to use up stale bread, year 'round.

Your freezer can help hold your next celebration. When making party foods, select do-ahead recipes. Consider making two cheese balls instead of one. Take one to the party, but keep its twin at home. It will await the **next** special occasion in your freezer.

Shopping Tips
Watch for sales on ingredients you regularly use. Then stock up!

Let someone else do the cooking. A deli-cooked chicken saves you about $1\frac{1}{2}$ hours and will keep, refrigerated, 3 to 5 days. This gives you options for assembling your own "home-cooked meals."

Purchase bagged, frozen boneless chicken breasts for your freezer. Defrost just what you need, as you need it, in the microwave.

When buying frozen foods, consider volume, calories, quality and price. Don't get caught just reaching for the "lite." Turn that package over and read the label.

Frozen vegetables are sometimes more nutritious than fresh. They are picked and flash-frozen, whereas "fresh" produce could be sitting around awhile.

Purchase low-sodium products if you are on a sodium-restricted diet. Instead, add a boost of flavor with fresh or dried herbs.

Look for already cleaned and sliced produce at the supermarket's deli or produce section: Mushrooms, celery, carrots, broccoli and cauliflower are popular ingredients.

Buying flowerets of broccoli or cauliflower for salads saves your prep time and there's no waste. But buy "by the bunch, not the pound," when purchasing whole, stem-on produce.

Shop for interesting and colorful vegetables to liven up your recipes. One is crinkle-cut carrots in the fresh produce or freezer section. Try "baby carrots" found in fresh produce. These are good in soups, casseroles, sautés and salads.

Buy bagged lettuce mixtures or baby spinach. It costs more but saves your time. Or save money by washing and drying (then bagging) your chosen lettuce in resealable plastic bags. Romaine stores well.

Shop the freshest: make your local farmers' market one of your shopping destinations. Your reward will be the hard-to-beat taste of summer — like tomatoes! Look for large beefsteak types for stuffing and slicing.

Need a fresh lemon but don't have one? Acquire a "plastic lemon" for the refrigerator. It's handy when you need just a little squirt of flavor.

Store potatoes in a cool, dark place — not in the refrigerator. Buy a quantity to last one to two weeks. Don't expect to keep them a month.

Look for reduced or lowered fat versions of dairy products. Be sure to buy dairy items before the "Sell Date" on the package. When selecting cheese, reach for your favorite or try a sharper or more robust variety. Then use **half** as much. (Many low and nonfat cheeses tend to lack taste and texture.)

Stock egg substitute in your freezer and never again worry about being out of fresh eggs. Just thaw in the microwave.

Maintaining Mix and Match Provisions

Substitution is the name of the game. Have a favorite sauce? Try using it another way. Interchange foods and flavors for quick recipes you already know by heart. Keep your cupboard stocked with all your favorites for more variety and to save time. Buy your regular products but begin using them in different ways.

Don't be afraid to "play with your food." Your own special addition of whatchamacallits will enhance any old stand-by or any new recipe. Experiment!

Dry packaged Italian salad dressing mix should be an essential in your kitchen. You can marinate with it — not using any oil! It's superb as a spice mixture. Sprinkle it (straight from the package) like you would a seasoning. And, of course, you can make salad dressing, then dress it up by adding sweet hot mustard and honey. Great flavor!

Speaking of dressings: Keep ready-made, bottled dressing in the refrigerator. It can do double duty and more: from salads to hot vegetables to meat marinades. Adapt Lisa's Italian Dressing to drizzle on cooked, cleaned deli (Dungeness) crab. It's fab! Try dipping or brushing dressings on French bread or toasted sourdough.

Taste tip: Lite sour cream and lite cream cheese products have more flavor than bland nonfat varieties. You might as well "go for it." Enjoy the rich taste. Although the fats differ, total calorie cost is nearly **equal**.

Use flavored breads for making stuffing for ham or pork as well as poultry.

Mix and match your leftovers to refresh a meal. Take leftover canned cranberries (please!). Use them in a different recipe or freeze to add to another dish.

Preparation ShortCuts
Quick tricks and techniques get you out of the kitchen faster. Try these.

Keep your miniprocessor or food processor easily accessible — always within reach. Remember, out of sight, out of mind. These appliances help cut down on prep and cleanup time.

Use a dull knife (like a table knife) to cut up ingredients right in their can when recipes call for something chopped. Works for everything from apricots to stewed tomatoes. Saves cleanup too!

For disposable mixing, use resealable plastic bags. You can store a main ingredient in it. Then later add other products to it, and shake or squish until mixed. Just make sure the seal is closed tightly. You can measure, mix and store several plastic bags of these dry mix-ups for your frequently used recipes. That's pantry-ready!

These handy storage bags are also ideal for microwaving frozen foods. In just a few minutes, you can easily defrost and heat directly in the bag (open it first for ventilation) using the microwave. This method gives you a head start on any side dish or casserole creation. (Be cautious when defrosting liquids in resealable plastic bags. They can spill. Be careful handling after you have heated in them. Both food and bag become very hot.)

For easier spreading, cream cheese or canned refried beans can be briefly heated in the microwave (remove from its container) on a paper plate.

For really short prep time, use already cleaned and cut vegetables from the produce section. Bring home cauliflower, mushrooms, carrots, celery, broccoli, cabbage — already sliced or diced.

When the recipe calls for ground chicken (or turkey), microwave two frozen chicken breasts, 10 to 12 minutes, covered. (Chicken is done when juices run clear after being pierced with a fork.) Let stand for 10 minutes. Cut into chunks and grind the cooked chicken in your miniprocessor.

Here's a timesaving tip that will also save you calories. Remove the skin from that cooled deli-cooked chicken. Hold the chicken part in one hand and use a paper towel (in the other hand) to grip and pull off the skin. The paper gives extra traction and keeps the skin from slipping. Remember: Safely discard bones away from pets.

If you like boxed or bagged stuffing mixes, shorten the cooking time by microwaving the recipe. Use nonfat broth or stock instead of water and bring it to a boil in the microwave. Add stuffing, then follow microwave cooking directions on the package.

To quick-cook four medium baking potatoes, pierce with a fork and microwave them on high for 10 to 15 minutes. Remove, wrap in foil and let stand another 5 to 10 minutes.

Like crisp baked potatoes but don't want to wait 45 minutes to an hour? Microwave them, then slip them into a conventional oven at 425° for about 10 minutes.

When boiling a potato, the smaller you cut it the faster it will cook but the more nutrients it will lose. Cutting small potatoes into halves is enough. If you bring the water to a boil first, then add the potatoes, they will be in contact with the water less time and retain more of their goodness.

Here's a quick way to prepare potatoes for a recipe requiring precooked: Wash and cut four potatoes (peeling is optional). Place in a microwaveable casserole or bowl with one-fourth cup water. Cover. Cook on high for 15 minutes or until tender.

Baking your chosen pizza base (like pita bread) first before adding sauce and toppings will give it a more pizza-like crisp crust.

Storing Ready-Meals — Your Freezer, Your Friend

Think of your freezer as your personal mini-market, only closer. Having something "ready to grab" at home saves your valuable time and an extra trip to the store.

Once again, **plan** on leftovers! While you are cooking, make more than you need for the meal. Create a refrigerated encore for the next day or "feed it to your freezer." It will return the favor!

For pasta, rice, even soups, a resealable plastic bag works well for storage. Release excess air and freeze flat. Takes up little precious space in your frozen cupboard.

Double a recipe and freeze it, like quiche. Wrap it well for its stay in the freezer and cook right from the frozen state (don't microwave in foil pie plates).

Cool down or freeze foods quickly to control bacterial growth. Store in airtight, moisture- and vapor-proof containers. Label packages with contents and date. Don't freeze too many items at once. You'll raise the temperature of the freezer above the recommended 0°.

Designate a shelf in the freezer for leftovers. Label, date and organize them so you won't forget about them.

When baking for the freezer, slightly undercook. Reserve top browning for when you reheat.

Use your freezer to take advantage of sales. Load up with bargain meats, vegetables, breads, but don't compromise on quality. What goes in must come out. Your deep freeze doesn't do make overs!

The best way to store extra bread is to freeze it. Refrigerating bread actually dries it out so "freeze it till you need it." Store pita bread this way for a quick pizza-mini.

Some produce shouldn't be put into cold storage. You don't want to refrigerate a raw potato. The starch will convert to sugar and this can cause browning in the center. Place in an open weave basket — in a dark cool place. Fifty degrees is ideal for storing spuds.

Keep seafood, like shrimp and imitation crab, recipe-ready in your freezer. They hold one month if properly wrapped and frozen.

If you are a dessert-lover, freeze a plain cake. Pound cake gives you a head start on your next dessert creation. It's versatile and goes with either fruit or chocolate flavors.

Reducing Cleanup

It seems like you can eat a meal faster than it takes you to make it and certainly quicker than it takes to clean up after it. Cut down on your cleanup time!

Mix, cook and serve in the same bowl or container, particularly with microwave recipes. Less used equals less to wash.

Use the same container and utensils throughout the recipe EXCEPT when preparing raw meat or poultry. (Cross contamination is a common cause of food-borne illness.)

Line the surface of cookware, like baking sheets, with foil. Recycle this where you can.

Use nonstick cooking spray and nonstick cookware. No more soaking and scrubbing.

Use that just emptied can to "measure" your next ingredient. Learn to gauge "by eye."

Learn to gauge teaspoon and tablespoon measurements. Once you know what a half-teaspoon looks like, you won't be washing measuring spoons each time.

There is no need to dirty a knife to separate a deli-cooked chicken. These are so tender, just gently break it apart once it has cooled.

Using precooked meats — like store-bought sausages or your own previously cooked and stored meats — saves a second cleanup. You won't have to sanitize a cutting board and knife like you must with raw meat.

A valuable shortcut to preparing a large meal or holiday dinner is using disposable or recyclable foil pans. Many have reinforced bottoms to hold extra weight. (Recycle.)

Items in **bold** type are recipe names.

A

almonds
  blanching, 80
  Turkey Almond Toss, 52
appetizers. See party foods, snacks, dips
apples, 162
  Apple Pie, 117-18
  Apple Sweet Potatoes, 122
artichoke hearts, 146
  Artichoke and Bean Salad, 22
  Artichoke Sauce, 176
  Cream Sauce, 178
asparagus, 62
  Five-A-Day Bouquet, 50

B

bacon, pieces, 51, 165
  on salad, 79
bacteria
  Cootie B-Gone, 10
  food safety, 10
  food storage, 69
barbecue sauce, 170
  Wow-ee! Bar-B-Que Sauce, 9
beans, 11, 146. See specific types
  Artichoke and Bean Salad, 22

Auntie Dolly's Ceci Pasta, 26
  dried, 152
  gas, 18
  potato stuffers, 102
  softening, 15
beef, 158
  Beefy Cover-Up Sauce, 177
  canned broth, 168
  horseradish, 170
  meatballs, 158
  Pasta Stir-Fry, 66
  substitute turkey, 159
beef, ground, 13
  Beefy Baker, 98
  Mexzanya, 14
beet juice
  Onion Flower, 38
berries. See also cranberries
  frozen, 171
biscuit mix, 152
  Heavenly Quiche, 64
black beans, 146
  Mexican-style salad, 7
  Southwest salad, 17
  Terrie's Special, Too, 97
bow-making, 140
bread, 152. See also cornbread
  freezing, 92
  frozen dough, 155
    used in pizza, 172
  label reading, 92
bread crumbs, 153, 165
bread, herbed
  stuffing, 115

breadsticks
  Italian Breadsticks, 91
broccoli, 59, 156
  Broccoli Blow-Out, 58
buns
  49'er Tightends, 90
  hotdog
    Italian Breadsticks, 91
burger. See beef, ground
butcher
  custom grind, 13
  turkey advice, 127
butter, 149
  pie crust, 118
  potatoes, 116
  stuffing, 115

C

cakes
  frozen, 172
  No-Pudge Fudge Cake, 108
  Peach Angel Cake, 22
calories
  burning, 111
  cutting, 3, 5, 13, 27, 49, 82, 85, 115-16, 146-7, 149, 151, 158-9, 169-70, 197
  snacking, 49
canned goods, 146
  exercise weights, 112
carrots, 157
  How Sweet It Is, 61
  Palm Tree Island, 36

- **FREE NEWSLETTER!** *Get time-saving shortcuts and delicious recipes featured on the popular television series. Just complete and mail the order form below.*

- **WEB SITE!** *Inside information about the show and the people who make it so much fun. Contest stuff too!*

    WWW.FASTCOOKING.COM

✂ -

Please send "The ShortCut Cook Express" newsletter — FREE.

Mail newsletter to:

    name: _____

    address: _____

    city, state, zip: _____

    phone: (_____) _____

Send newsletter request to: **"The ShortCut Cook," 785 Oak Grove Road #E-2, Concord, CA 94518.**

212

To order "Beat the Clock Cooking" by mail

(A portion of the proceeds goes to food assistance programs.)

Please send me _____ copies of "Beat the Clock Cooking" at $18.95 each plus shipping.
(Please allow 6-8 weeks for delivery.)

$18.95 x ____ books = $	
$3.95 shipping x ____ books = $	
CA residents add $1.56 x ____ books = $	
TOTAL = $	

Please make check or money order payable to: **TeriLee Productions, Inc.**
Send to: **"The ShortCut Cook," 785 Oak Grove Road #E-2, Concord, CA 94518.**

Mail cookbook(s) to: _____

(Please print clearly)   _____

                            _____   ✂

- -

Please send me _____ copies of "Beat the Clock Cooking" at $18.95 each plus shipping.
(Please allow 6-8 weeks for delivery.)

$18.95 x ____ books = $	
$3.95 shipping x ____ books = $	
CA residents add $1.56 x ____ books = $	
TOTAL = $	

Please make check or money order payable to: **TeriLee Productions, Inc.**
Send to: **"The ShortCut Cook," 785 Oak Grove Road #E-2, Concord, CA 94518.**

Mail cookbook(s) to: _____

(Please print clearly)   _____

                            _____